T
N
C
T
R
S

Check Out Receipt

Chicago Bee

Friday, August 18,
2017 2:01:37 PM

Item: R033552563
Title: Going in style
Due: 08/25/2017

Item: R043110488 1
Title: Smart women
protect their assets :
essential information
for every woman about
wills, trusts, and more
Due: 09/08/2017

Total items: 2

Thank You!

136

SMART WOMEN PROTECT THEIR ASSETS

Essential Information for Every Woman About **Wills**, **Trusts**, and **More**

WYNNE A. WHITMAN

Vice President, Publisher: Tim Moore
Associate Publisher and Director
of Marketing: Amy Neidlinger
Executive Editor: Jim Boyd
Editorial Assistant: Myesha Graham
Development Editor: Russ Hall
Operations Manager: Gina Kanouse
Digital Marketing Manager: Julie Phifer
Publicity Manager: Laura Czaja

Assistant Marketing Manager: Megan Colvin
Cover Designer: Chuti Prasertsith
Managing Editor: Kristy Hart
Project Editor: Betsy Harris
Copy Editor: Harrison Ridge Services
Proofreader: Williams Woods Publishing Services
Indexer: Jovana San Nicolas-Shirley
Compositor: Nonie Ratcliff
Manufacturing Buyer: Dan Uhrig

FT Press offers excellent discounts on this book when ordered in quantity for bulk purchases or special sales. For more information, please contact U.S. Corporate and Government Sales, 1-800-382-3419, corpsales@pearsontechgroup.com. For sales outside the U.S., please contact International Sales at international@pearson.com.

ISBN-10: 0-13-236040-3
ISBN-13: 978-0-13-236040-1

Pearson Education LTD.
Pearson Education Australia PTY, Limited.
Pearson Education Singapore, Pte. Ltd.
Pearson Education North Asia, Ltd.
Pearson Education Canada, Ltd.
Pearson Educatión de Mexico, S.A. de C.V.
Pearson Education—Japan
Pearson Education Malaysia, Pte. Ltd.

Library of Congress Cataloging-in-Publication Data

Whitman, Wynne A.
   Smart women protect their assets : essential information for every woman about wills, trusts, and more / Wynne A. Whitman. — 1st ed.
      p. cm.
   ISBN 0-13-236040-3 (pbk. : alk. paper) 1. Estate planning—United States—Popular works.
2. Tax planning—United States—Popular works. 3. Women—Legal status, laws, etc. I. Title.
   KF750.Z9W52 2008
   332.024'0160820973—dc22
                                    2008026758

*To Mom, Dad, and Stacy for their continuing
support and encouragement.*

Contents

1

Chapter 10: How Do You Talk to Your Loved Ones About Your Death? ... 151

What Should You Do Next? ... 156

Chapter 11: What Should You Do in Special Situations? ... 157

Successful Singles ... 157

Homemakers ... 158

Widows ... 159

Generous Grandmothers ... 159

Divorcées ... 160

Cohabiters ... 161

Lesbians ... 162

Caregivers ... 162

Heiresses ... 163

What Should You Do Next? ... 164

Chapter 12: What Happens If You Are Appointed as a Fiduciary? ... 165

What Should You Do Next? ... 171

Conclusion: Estate Planning Checklist ... 173

Suggested Resources ... 185

Glossary ... 187

Index ... 197

Acknowledgments

My thanks begin with Jim Boyd, who had faith in my ability to write "my own book" and encouraged me to take on this project from day one. I'm also indebted to the entire team at Pearson and FT Press for their understanding and support: Russ Hall, Betsy Harris, Todd Taber, Julie Phifer, Laura Czaja, Megan Colvin, and the entire hard-working team, as well as Linda Harrison for her copy-editing genius. I'd also be remiss if I didn't acknowledge Doris S. Michaels and her agency for their assistance.

I also have to send out big "Thank Yous!" to the many incredible, smart women I've worked with, both as colleagues and clients, for their insights and for being constant and consistent sources of inspiration. This includes the many friends and strangers, alike, who completed surveys and shared their stories (and fears) about estate planning. Thank you!

Personal gratitude goes out to many: Mary Joan K. Sheridan Kennedy, Jeremy Pearce, Betsy Phillips, Wendy Bandrowski, Jeff Bandrowski, Lynn Sharp, Carolyn Remmey, and April Mattikow. Last, but certainly not least, my continued gratitude to my parents and my sister for supporting this, and all projects; their talented editing and innovative ideas; and most of all their love and thoughtfulness. And of course, big thanks go to Wee Whit, Reese, and Jamie—the motivating forces behind much brilliant planning!

About the Author

Wynne A. Whitman, J.D., M.B.A., LL.M., is a tax, Trusts, and estates attorney in New Jersey. Every day she answers clients' questions and assists them in putting their legal affairs in order, whether it's a young couple worrying about providing for their kids or an older widow who wants to make sure her loved ones get every penny possible. Wynne also assists in administering the estates of loved ones and knows first hand that a well-planned estate is an invaluable gift to those left behind.

Wynne is the coauthor of *Wants, Wishes, and Wills: A Medical and Legal Guide to Protecting Yourself and Your Family in Sickness and in Health* (Financial Times Press, May 2007), as well as *Shacking Up: The Smart Girl's Guide to Living in Sin Without Getting Burned* (Broadway Books, March 2003), which discusses the social and legal implications of cohabitation. With her sister, Stacy Whitman, Wynne has also ghostwritten four health and fitness books for two nationally recognized celebrities.

Introduction

Let's face it, none of us want to think about getting older. (Though one look in the mirror usually makes it hard not to!) And, we certainly don't want to think or talk about dying, especially when there's so much more living to do. At the same time, though, we all want some control over how we spend our final days, how we protect all we've worked for, and who gets our money and most prized possessions. But if you don't act *now*, while you're still alive and kicking, you could lose your opportunity to make those all-important choices.

I'll be the first to admit: The topic of estate planning isn't fun or sexy. Even I would rather sip a glass of Sauvignon Blanc and curl up with a good John Grisham book than sit around talking about Wills. But, it's necessary to do it if you want to have a say in what happens to you and your belongings in the event of a worst case scenario. That's where this book can really help.

Smart Women Protect Their Assets is written specifically for women like you, who are looking for straightforward advice tailored just for them. Because I know how intimidating and scary the subject matter can be, I'm here to make it understandable and approachable. And, with any luck, I might just get you to crack a smile now and again.

An effective estate plan isn't just writing a Will and calling it a day. It's making decisions today, while you still can, about your health care and finances—in case you lose the ability to manage them yourself. It's also about providing peace of mind to your loved ones by being organized and letting them know exactly what it is you want. It's about having the strength to discuss tough issues with your husband, partner, or significant other. It's understanding what's right for you and also what's right for your loved ones.

Estate planning involves asking one question after another. Each chapter in *Smart Women Protect Their Assets* answers each of these questions. You'll learn why estate planning is important in Chapter 1, "Why Should You Worry About Estate Planning?" and how to calculate your net worth in Chapter 2, "What Exactly Does Your Estate Include?" Taxes, taxes, taxes, and more taxes are explained in Chapter 3, "Is It Really *That* Important to Think About Taxes?" (and I promise, you'll stay awake while you read it!). We all know that as much as we think we can do it alone, we need help from friends and family. Chapter 4, "Who Makes Sure Everything You Want to Have Happen Happens When You're Gone?" outlines who does what when you're gone to be sure what you want to have happen, well...happens.

Your heartstrings will be tugged in Chapter 5, "What Will Happen to Your Loved Ones?" as we discuss your loved ones and what you can do for them. Then, of course, there's the meat and potatoes of our discussion, actually putting your plan into place, which is covered in Chapter 6, "What's a Will? What's a Trust? How Do You Use Them to Put Your Plan in Place?" Then, because we all love fancy things, you'll learn how to dress up your planning in Chapter 7, "What If You Want to Get Fancy with Your Planning?"

It's also important to select individuals to help you if you're ever unable to act for yourself. You'll learn why in Chapter 8, "What If You Get Sick and Can't Make Decisions?" But your planning requires more than legal documents, which is explained in Chapter 9, "Is There Anything Else You Should Do to Be Prepared?" And, because it's tough to even read about death, you'll get ideas about how to talk about the subject with your family when you turn to Chapter 10, "How Do You Talk to Your Loved Ones About Your Death?"

In addition to comprehensive, easy-to-understand answers to your questions, *Smart Women Protect Their Assets* gives you creative solutions to common problems, such as a child who can't manage money, kids who just can't get along, or a disabled grandchild. Every single one of you has your own challenges and issues. Whether you're a single mom, an unmarried 40-something, a recent divorcee, or a loving grandmother, you'll find information geared specifically toward you in Chapter 11, "What Should You Do in Special Situations?" You'll learn what to do, but also what *not* to do. There's a lot of misinformation out there—*Smart Women Protect Their Assets* lets you know what works, what doesn't, and the scare tactics to dismiss. Because there may be a day you're called upon to act as an Executor or Trustee, you'll learn about your responsibilities in Chapter 12, "What Happens If You Are Appointed as a Fiduciary?" This book provides you with the information you need to create the best plan for you and your loved ones. And to help you get started, there's a comprehensive checklist in the Conclusion to give you an easy to follow To Do list.

Keep in mind, though, that this book is designed to give you ideas about estate planning. It is not a substitute for hands-on legal and financial counsel. It is also not a book about elder law or planning for individuals with a disability who are concerned about eligibility for government benefits. Those areas are unique practices of law and are not addressed in this book. There's a lot you can do on your own; but because your situation is unique, you need your own attorney to assist you in preparing legal documents that will help you accomplish your goals. By being informed and prepared before you step foot into your lawyer's office, you can save yourself quite a bit of time (and maybe some legal fees as well).

Because the IRS loves to make my life complicated, as well as yours, please read the following disclaimer required by IRS Circular 230 before proceeding:

Unless otherwise expressly approved in advance by the author, any discussion of federal tax matters herein is not intended and cannot be used 1) to avoid penalties under the federal tax laws, or 2) to promote, market or recommend to another party any transaction or tax-related matter addressed herein.

I challenge each one of you to stop running from the issues and instead to tackle them head on. Have some fun making decisions. If fun just isn't going to happen, at least think about how great you'll feel knowing you've protected your assets!

Chapter 1

Why Should You Worry About Estate Planning?

D*eath.* It isn't the kind of thing that anyone likes to think about, much less discuss. Even an episode of *Grey's Anatomy*, when its fictional character is "checking out," is enough to make many of us well up with tears or cover our eyes and shudder. Death is morbid and distressing; it's also a fact of life. We'll all die one day. And then what?

That's when things get really confusing and complicated. There's much to do: paperwork, taxes, retirement plan rollovers, insurance policies, and more paperwork—not to mention lots of legal and financial mumbo jumbo. True, you could do nothing and let your loved ones deal with the mess when you're gone. However, if you're like most women, that's the last thing you want to do. Whether you have a husband, children, siblings, or aging parents, chances are you spend a good deal of time caring for others. Why would you want to do any differently in death?

Women today aren't just caregivers. We're entre-
preneurs, successful professionals, and savvy investors.
(Remember, we can bring home the bacon and fry it up
in a pan!) We control more than half the private wealth
in the United States. We outlive our male partners, on
average, by four to seven years. We need to be aware of
what we have and what we want to do with it. We're in
control of ourselves, our bodies, and our minds. We also
need to be in control of our pocketbooks and what we
do with them at the end of our lives.

Women and Property

For many centuries a woman's only legal possession
was her dowry (the money and property that she
brought to her husband in marriage—think fancy hope
chest filled with silver and china!). Some women,
depending on their social stature and place of residence, could control their dowry. In some European
countries, the groom managed the dowry along with
his assets. Often, a woman had no control over anything; she couldn't even sell her old hoop dress without her husband's consent! Thankfully, laws began to
change in sixth-century Europe. A husband was able to
administer, but not sell, his better half's property.
Next, the concept of his and her separate estates soon
took hold both in England and the United States. The
legal right of *primogeniture*, which provided that only
the eldest son inherited the family estate, was soon
abolished. (That took long enough!) Soon, women
were granted dower rights (different from her dowry),
which guaranteed a bride some part of her groom's
estate if he died first. For the first time, women could

be independent property owners, both during and after their husband's death. To protect widows from being *disinherited* (left no money or property) by their deceased husbands, dower rights remained in effect for many years, often providing that the widow receive one-half or one-third of his estate, depending upon whether there were children from the marriage, if she was "cut out" of the Will. Today, in many states in our country, women are protected from disinheritance with their right to an "elective share" of their husband's estate, often at least one-third of his estate. But don't think it's only us gals the law protects; husbands are entitled to the same elective share. Of course, if you've signed a pre- or ante-nuptial agreement, the elective share laws may not apply. No wonder the Donald Trump types always have pre-nups!

Why You Need to Plan

Unfortunately, you need more than good intentions to have your wishes carried out. When the law is involved, telling your loved ones what you want means nothing—and that doesn't even consider the miscommunications that can occur when you fail to put something in writing. I had the great honor of clerking for two distinguished jurists my first year after law school. The most important thing I learned was that there are always three versions of every event: yours, mine, and what actually happened. We all perceive and remember things differently. Why leave your intentions open to misinterpretations when you can record exactly what you want in an estate plan?

Why Wise Women Plan

My father died at my feet the day before my wedding. He was 58 years old. Fortunately, he had all his "ducks in order" as far as his Will and his Trust Fund, so I always felt it was the smartest thing to do to be prepared for one's death.—*Anderson, age 50*

You need to identify your wishes ahead of time so in the event of death or catastrophic illness, your wishes are met.—*Julie, age 42*

My husband and I are working together with a professional financial planner and attorney to ensure that our assets, insurance, debt, etc., are properly managed so in the event of our deaths, our children will be able to continue in the best manner possible, as close to the standard of living they currently enjoy, without horrible tax repercussions.—*Missy, age 38*

A few years ago I walked alongside a dear friend who was dying of cancer at age 39. Literally, the last time he left the house was to go to the lawyers to make sure everything was updated, signed, and ready for his departure. The last time I saw him up on the computer was to type out advice to his wife about their financial assets and his ideas for her future investments. Once this was all "put to bed," he was able to go to bed, and died a number of days later. Of course, I have learned from all this that it's MUCH MUCH better to have all of this in place before a crisis comes.—*Jennie, age 41*

The federal government takes a huge percentage of estates that aren't properly planned. I want to make the decisions about where my money/things go, not the state or the federal government.—*Jill, age 43*

Estate planning is very important in order to care for one's family; it decreases emotional trauma following the death of a loved one by simplifying and clarifying issues, and it ensures that your personal assets go directly to your loved ones.—*Faye, age 32*

I've seen the effects that a lack of estate planning can bring, with my grandmother losing almost half of the value of her assets to the government.—*Addie, age 38*

What do I mean when I say telling your loved ones means nothing? We live in a society governed by laws. These laws are designed to protect us, which includes protecting our assets when we're no longer living. When you die, your loved ones can't simply walk up to your banker and say, "Mom has died. Can you divide the assets among the children?" If only it were that simple! Regulations and other rules require your local banker to prove that you are, in fact, deceased. To do this, your loved ones can simply provide a death certificate. But there's more. The banker must be sure that the person making the request has the legal authority to do so. This legal authority is usually conferred by a local court after your Will is admitted to probate (more on probate in Chapter 6, "What's a Will? What's a Trust? How Do You Use Them to Put Your Plan in Place?"). The person who receives the authority is the **Executor** or **Personal Representative** you've named in your Will. Or, maybe the banker needs a copy of an original Trust document showing who serves as Trustee if your assets are titled in the name of a Trust. Regardless, you have the power to give this authority to act to someone after your passing. If you've left no Will, the Court will appoint an individual to be the Administrator or Personal Representative of your estate—and it won't necessarily be the person you would have chosen.

Intestacy 101

When you don't have a Will or Trust that spells out who should inherit your house, your car, your wedding ring, and all your other precious belongings, or when you have assets that don't pass by beneficiary designation or to a joint tenant, the laws of the state in which you live decide who receives your most prized possessions. Each state is different, with different determinations as to who receives what. If you have your own ideas in mind (which I guarantee almost all of you do!), you need to document them in a Will or Trust.

If none of your family members, friends, or other trusted associates is deemed to have the legal authority to act on your behalf, it's likely that you've died intestate. Dying **intestate** means that you've left no Will naming an Administrator or Personal Representative for your estate. If so, in most states, the law will determine who that individual should be. Often, the authority is granted to a surviving spouse, or, if you're unmarried or widowed, to your children, or if you have no children, to a parent or sibling. Chances are, these are the individuals you'd want to carry out your final wishes and handle all the paperwork and legal whatnot. But what if you were on the brink of divorce from your husband? Or your kids can't balance a checkbook let alone file tax returns?

Equally important is what happens to your property if you die intestate. In the Sunshine State (Florida), if you're married and die without a Will—and you don't have any children, grandchildren, or great-grandchildren (otherwise known as descendants)—your husband would receive anything that doesn't have a beneficiary designation or isn't a survivorship account. If you're married and have descendants that are also your husband's, he'd receive the first $60,000, plus half of your remaining estate; your descendants would receive the other half. If your descendants are *not* your husband's descendants, your descendants would receive half and your husband the other half. If you're not married, your assets pass to your descendants, and if you don't have any, to your parents. If your parents aren't living, your assets go to your siblings or their descendants, and if none, to your grandparents or their children (your aunts and uncles), then to your cousins, and then to the "kin of your last deceased spouse" (that means step-children or in-laws!). Finally, if you have no living relatives, your estate passes to the State of Florida to be used for the state's school fund.

In my home state, New Jersey, the laws of intestacy are a lot like Florida's, with several notable exceptions.

First, if you're a registered domestic partner in New Jersey (New Jersey allows homosexual couples and unmarried couples over the age of 62 to register as domestic partners), your domestic partner is treated as a spouse. Second, if you're survived by a husband and no descendants, your groom receives the first 25 percent of your estate (but not less than $50,000 or more than $200,000) plus three-quarters of the balance of your estate, with your mom and dad getting the rest. If your folks aren't living, your husband gets it all. Third, if you don't have any living relatives, then your step-children or their descendants will receive your estate. What some of you may find disturbing is that these step-children don't have to be your last husband's kids.

Here's an example: Remember your delinquent step-son from your first marriage to what's-his-name? You know, the one who has never held a steady job, used to sleep (and drool!) on your couch, and once spent time in the slammer for peddling drugs? Depending on where you live, he could technically get a slice of your pie if you died intestate and aren't survived by a husband, children, grandkids, parents, and other living blood relatives. While the scenario may sound far-fetched (especially if you have a big brood that's likely to survive you), it just goes to show that it's in your best interest to draw up the necessary documents so you can be absolutely certain of where your money will end up.

Escheat—Is That A New Expression for Internet Cheating?

Good guess, but no. **Escheat** refers to assets that are transferred to the state in which you reside when someone leaves behind unclaimed property. Unclaimed property can be an income tax refund that was returned to Uncle Sam as undeliverable or a bank account you forgot when you graduated college. Property can also escheat to your state when you die without a Will or Trust and have no living relatives.

Worse, for many people, than *who* receives your assets as a result of intestacy is *what* happens to the funds for your small children if you die without a Will or Trust. In New Jersey, the funds for a minor child are held by a local court in a minor's account. First, the court controls and invests the assets. They do a terrific job, but it seems to me an investment professional might be able to make those funds grow a little bit more because they have more flexibility in selecting investments. Second, and the most frightening of all, is that your children will receive their share of your estate *at age 18*! In all my years of estate planning, I've yet to meet a client who thinks her children would be able to handle large sums of money at 18. If you plan, you can have the money for your wee ones held in trust to any age or ages you would like. Talk about incentive to start your **estate planning** today!

The Worst Reasons Not to Think About Your Estate Plan

Trust me, I hear lots of excuses from women. Here are some of my favorites:

1. *As soon as I write my Will, something bad will happen.* Sorry, but in all my years of experience I've yet to see a client sign her Will and then drop dead. This excuse is just silly.

2. *My husband takes care of business things.* Hello??? Welcome to the twenty-first century! Your husband can't write a Will for you, and more importantly, these are important decisions that YOU need to make. It's time to step up to the plate and take charge of your own affairs.

3. *Nothing's going to happen to me; my grandmother lived to 108.* That's wonderful...but don't forget that terrible things happen every day. You can't count on Grandma Greta's golden years to be yours too.

4. *I don't own a house or anything of significant value, so why do I need a Will?* Even if your means are modest, I guarantee that there is something you have that you want to pass on in a particular way. Only estate planning will help you do that. If nothing else, you'll save your loved ones a lot of time and grief by putting your desires in writing.

5. *It's too sad. I just can't deal with it.* Please. As my favorite cocktail napkin says, "Put on your big girl pants and deal with it."

The key to all of this is you—what you want to do and what you want to have happen when you die. I thought about the best way to get this point across and

> *An inheritance is a gift, not an entitlement. Don't let anyone tell you otherwise.*

decided that there is no sugar-coating my message: You need to be proactive to achieve *your* goals. And I repeat, *your* goals. As you continue to read this, remember that your estate plan is your plan. There is no need for guilt, angst, or any one of those other complexes we, as women, are particularly good at feeling. Create the plan that reflects what you want. Period.

We've all heard horror stories about greedy children denying proper care to an ailing parent so they can get their inheritances or ne'er-do-well in-laws circling the dying matriarch waiting for their share of the pot. While that still may happen, what actually happens is up to you. Let the vultures hover all they want. If you have a plan in place, your plan remains in place even if you become incapacitated. In the unfortunate event of crooks who trick unsuspecting, incapacitated women into changing their plan (it happens more than you can imagine), if you have a prior plan in place, a court should hold that the prior documents prevail.

Who You're Planning For

While I've talked (probably too much) about doing what you want, think about who you're planning for. It's not only for you. It's for your loved ones. You're working hard to be sure that they're taken care of. For some of you, your beneficiaries aren't people, but charitable institutions that you wish to support after your death. Regardless of whom or what you want to provide for, you need an estate plan that includes them. If you don't, your assets could end up being distributed according to state law. Chances are most of you wouldn't want someone else to decide who gets to keep your mother's wedding ring or your treasured teacup collection. Now, if that's not enough to scare you into action, I don't know what is! Chapter 5, "What Will Happen to Your Loved Ones?" discusses the many different beneficiaries and the planning options for each. You can be creative. I'll show you how to work your creativity into your plan to achieve your goals, protect your assets, and care for your loved ones.

How to Get Started

As my favorite song from *The Sound of Music* goes, "Let's start at the very beginning. A very good place to start." So, what is the very beginning of estate planning? It's finding a lawyer specializing in estate planning to implement your goals into an effective plan. Why do you need a specialist? You need a specialist for the same reason you don't see an orthopedic surgeon when you have a skin rash or a podiatrist when you have chronic headaches. Like medicine, the law is filled with experts in a multitude of different areas. You don't want a criminal lawyer who usually defends murderers to write your Trust or a patent attorney to plan your estate.

A very good place to start your search for an estate planning attorney is to ask your family, friends, financial planners, advisors, and other colleagues for a referral. Without a doubt, a word-of-mouth referral is extremely helpful. Another option is to call your state or local bar association to see if they have a referral service. Legal Aid offices are also available if you can't afford a private practice attorney. Not only should the attorney you select be a specialist in the area of estate planning, he or she should also be licensed to practice law in the state in which you reside because an expert in Pennsylvania isn't necessarily an expert in Idaho. Still can't find someone to help guide you through the planning process? Log onto one of these Web sites:

- **American Bar Association Lawyer Locator (www.abanet.org/lawyerlocator/searchlawyer. html)**—Search members of the ABA by specialty, including Trusts and estates.

- **American College of Trust and Estate Counsel (www.actec.org)**—Well-versed in all areas of estate planning, ACTEC fellows are accredited practitioners with at least ten years of experience in this area of the law.

- **Martindale-Hubbell Lawyer Locator (www. martindale.com)**—This database allows you to search by specialty, including searching by Trusts and estates and geographic area.

- **National Academy of Elder Law Attorneys (www.naela.com)**—NAELA members focus on the needs of elderly and disabled individuals.

When you call to make an appointment with a prospective counselor (hint, hint), inquire about costs, expertise, and availability. While I'm the first one to advise you that good planning is more than worth the money, and then some, you have to be comfortable with the likely fees. Preparing estate planning documents shouldn't be done on a flat fee basis—an estate plan is never cookie-cutter or boilerplate and shouldn't be priced as if it were an all-inclusive Caribbean vacation. Make sure your attorney can get your estate planning documents completed on a timely basis. The best lawyer in the world isn't the best if the work doesn't get finished. Make clear your expectations for completion. It's important to ask questions now, before you've invested in an attorney. If you don't like the answers or the responsiveness, get a second opinion.

When's Your Date with the Grim Reaper?

No, I'm not talking about my last blind date. (That's a story for another book!) Instead, I'm talking about life's uncertainties. You just don't know when the Grim Reaper will come calling. (Men—always so unpredictable!) I'm not trying to keep you from sleeping at night; I'm simply reminding you that life can be cruel, unfair, and inconvenient. We don't know when tragedy might strike, so it's best to plan for it today. Don't add to your already stressed and multitasked life by waiting until the day before you have surgery scheduled or an overseas business trip to put your affairs in order. The last thing you want to do is stop by your lawyer's office on the way to the airport or to have your attorney visit you in the emergency room. (Believe me, I wouldn't want anyone who isn't my nearest and dearest to see me in one of those oh-so-attractive hospital gowns!)

Studies show that fewer than 30 percent of Americans have estate planning documents in place. We're an aging population. We need to think about these things and think about them today. I applaud you for taking the first step in taking control of your planning and protecting your assets. I hope I make the process less intimidating (with a little laughter here and there) to encourage you to get it done. Talking about estate planning and the end of life isn't exactly a walk in the park. But, control (at least for me!) provides the peace of mind to enjoy that walk in the park, and having an organized estate plan gives you that control.

What Should You Do Next?

1. Ask friends, family, professionals, and colleagues for an attorney referral.
2. Call and make an appointment!

Chapter 2

What Exactly Does Your Estate Include?

*E*state. Sounds dramatic, doesn't it? If you're like me, the first things you think of are rolling hills and a mile-long tree-lined driveway leading to a palatial homestead. But in the world of estate planning, your estate is much different. Your **estate**, quite simply, is everything you own at the time of death. And yes, I mean *everything*, from the money in your bank accounts to your car to the sterling silver passed down from your great aunt.

Why Is Knowing Exactly What You Have So Important?

As you'll learn in Chapter 3, "Is It Really *That* Important to Think About Taxes?" estate taxes are calculated based on what you own, or are entitled to, at your death. Inheritance taxes, generally, are calculated and imposed on whoever inherits from your estate. Knowing what you have, or have the right to, how it's owned, what it's worth, and what your beneficiary designations say is critical to implementing your estate plan.

Assets and How They're Owned

Your estate is comprised of your assets. There are five basic asset categories. As we go through each one, start making a list of what you own, what it's worth, and with whom you own the property. There is a sample list (also called a Net Worth Statement) near the end of this chapter to help you make notes.

1. **Real property—Real property** includes any house, townhouse, condominium, as well as vacation property or timeshare that you own or co-own. It also includes vacant land, farm land, and commercial properties. Make a list of all the property you own and where it's located. If you know the approximate current value, include the value on the list. If you don't know the current value, you can obtain an appraisal or make an educated guess based on recent local real estate sales (available online). The assessed value is usually not a good indicator of your property's fair market value because several years may have passed since your property received a formal assessment. List under liabilities any debt you have on the real property. This could be a mortgage or outstanding home equity line of credit. If you can find a copy of the Deed, this will help you determine how you own the property (either alone or with someone else). Include this information on your list as well.

Asset Analysis

Real property—Land and whatever is attached to the land.

Personal property—Art, antiques, vehicles, furniture, photographs, jewelry, paintings, and collections. In other words, everything you can touch and feel.

Intangible property—Stocks, securities, business interests, patents, bank accounts, copyrights, and all other financial investments.

Property you can control—Assets you can control by exercising a power of appointment, usually through a Trust. These may be included in your estate for estate tax purposes (not everyone has this type of asset).

Assets with a beneficiary designation—Any assets that allow you to complete a form (beneficiary designation) that states who receives the asset when you die. The most common examples are life insurance, retirement accounts, and payable on death accounts.

2. **Personal property**—One of the hardest things to value is your **personal property**. Most of us love our things even though they wouldn't fetch much at an estate auction or even a garage sale, while others may have prized collections or beautiful antiques worth much more than you could even imagine. Over the years, I have had the great pleasure of hearing Carolyn Remmey, of Remmey Antiques and Fine Art, New Vernon, New Jersey, speak on the subject of personal

property. She's given me a great deal of insight into the value our personal property can have, whether it's a piece of jewelry, a set of antique chairs, or a civil war key bucket. Look at the "stuff" you have. Is any of it of particular value? Maybe it's a Revolutionary War era painting you inherited from your Uncle George. If you're unsure as to the value of certain items, ask an expert for an appraisal. If you have the property insured through a rider on your insurance policy, you may already have had an appraisal completed. Don't forget to include the items in your garage. Cars, boats, and motor homes all count as personal property assets.

If Your Name's On It, You Own It, Right?

You do own it, that's right. But, you may not own all of it. How an asset is titled is important in estate planning because certain forms of ownership determine what and how you may pass an asset at death.

Joint tenants—Joint tenancy assets pass on death to the surviving joint tenants, regardless of what a Will or Trust might say. Real estate and bank and brokerage accounts can be held as **joint tenants**. There can even be more than one joint tenant. You've probably heard of a joint checking account. This is the most common example of a joint tenancy asset. If you see the letters JT TEN (Joint Tenants) or JTWROS (Joint Tenants with Right of Survivorship) listed on the account, it's a joint tenancy account.

Tenancy by the entirety—A joint tenancy asset that can only exist between a husband and wife. Usually, **tenancy by the entirety** properties are limited to real estate.

Tenants-in-common—Real estate or bank or brokerage accounts owned as **tenants-in-common** have multiple tenants, but no right of survivorship. On the death of a tenant, his or her share of the asset passes according to his or her Will. A tenant-in-common doesn't own a particular part of the asset (let's say the backyard and garage), but instead owns a partial interest in the whole property. Any asset owned as a joint tenant can also be owned as tenants-in-common (think real estate and bank accounts). A tenancy-in-common account usually has the designation TEN COM or JT TIC.

Individual assets—If an asset is in your name alone and has no beneficiary designation, it's an individual asset that will be distributed as you direct in your Will or Trust. Examples include checking accounts, real property, stocks, cars, and business interests.

Assets with a beneficiary designation—Many assets, such as life insurance, retirement accounts, annuities, savings bonds, and certificates of deposit, have beneficiary designations. For many of these assets, the beneficiary designation takes precedence over your Will. It's important to review these designations to be sure that they are consistent with your estate plan and don't name someone who has already died or is, perhaps, no longer a part of your life.

Payable on death assets—Payable on death (POD) accounts list a beneficiary who gets the asset when you die. POD accounts are seen the most often with savings bonds and bank accounts. Be sure to tell your attorney if you have any substantial assets that already have POD designations; these assets will be distributed as designated, no matter what your Will says.

Community property—Property obtained during marriage in one of the nine community property states (Arizona, California, Idaho, Louisiana, Nevada, New Mexico, Texas, Washington, and Wisconsin) is owned by both husband and wife, with each spouse owning "an undivided one-half interest" in the entire asset. In Alaska, you can elect that your property be treated as community property. At death, the surviving spouse receives one half of the community property; the spouse that has died may dispose of his or her share by Will. For example, if you live in a community property state and have a bank account (in your name only) with $10,000, one-half belongs to your husband. Only your $5,000 will pass as you direct in your Will or Trust.

If you don't know how an asset is titled—ask! Talk to your lawyer, broker, financial advisor, or bank manager for guidance. To quote Martha Stewart, "It's a good thing" to ask for help.

3. **Intangible property—**I'm sure just the thought of wading through file boxes of paperwork is enough for most of you to put this book down and pick up a book that's a lot more fun. But I'm

going to give you a great tip to get started in identifying your assets. While it might take a little digging, it will make this project much easier: Find last year's income tax return. Why? On Schedule B, you're required to list the accounts that pay you interest and dividends. For example, on Schedule B you'll find a list of all the banks that pay you interest, as well as the companies or brokerage firms that pay you dividends. This likely means that you have accounts at these firms or shares of stock in the listed companies. This is your **intangible property**. If you can't find monthly or quarterly statements with the current value of the account, stop by your local branch or place a call to the toll-free customer service number to get a copy. Next, see if there are any Forms K-1 attached to your tax return. A K-1 notes the income you received from a business, partnership, or other entity (such as a Trust or estate). This might help jog your memory about other business interests you have. If you have a good accountant, ask him or her to help you out. It may save you lots of time digging through dusty

My impression is that as a married person, all of our assets are jointly owned, so if either of us dies, the other wouldn't have to deal with much red tape. If we BOTH die, however, we're screwed. —Bonnie, age 39

documents. Include each account on your asset list, as well as its current value. Assets with a beneficiary designation are discussed below, but because many intangible assets can also have a beneficiary designation, make sure to note if there is a beneficiary designation associated with any account or asset or if the account or asset is held jointly with another person.

4. **Property you can control**—Many women are fortunate to be the **beneficiary** of a Trust established by a grandparent, husband, or other family member. Each Trust likely has unique terms, but all will include specifics on how income is paid and principal used for the beneficiary. Many Trusts also include language regarding a power of appointment. A **power of appointment** allows a beneficiary, whether during her lifetime or at her death, to direct the distribution of the Trust principal. These powers can be general (the funds can be distributed to anyone, including the beneficiary's creditors) or limited (for example, distributions may only be made to the descendants of the beneficiary or the individual who established the Trust). It's important to determine if you have this power in the event you would like to direct exactly where the proceeds pass on your death. It's also critical to understand what kind of power you have in determining the size of your estate. A *limited* power of appointment does not result in the value of the Trust being included in your estate; but a *general* power of appointment results in the full value of the Trust being

included in your estate for estate tax purposes. In other words, if you are receiving the income from a Trust worth $1,000,000 and have a general power of appointment, the full $1,000,000 is included in your estate for estate tax purposes—something both you and your attorney need to know.

5. **Assets with a beneficiary designation**—If you're shaking your head wondering what a **beneficiary designation** is, it's a form that allows you to name, or designate, the individual or entities to receive a particular asset when you start pushing up daisies. Many assets or accounts, such as individual retirement accounts, retirement plans, annuities, life insurance and payable-on-death (POD) accounts, have beneficiary designations. The beneficiary designation takes effect regardless of what your Will or Trust might state. What happens if there is no beneficiary named or your beneficiary has died? The beneficiary becomes your estate and your Will, if you have one, determines who gets the goods.

That's why it's so important to double-check your beneficiary designations. Review your files. If you can't find a copy of the designations you've completed, place a call to your financial planner, banker, human resources representative, broker, life insurance agent, or any institution you have an account with to get a copy. Even if you have a copy of a beneficiary designation, double check that it's the most current form on file. In this day of continuous mergers and acquisitions, forms get lost, misplaced, or misfiled. (This has happened to me on numerous occasions.) Make sure the designation you want is in the hands of the right people and that it has been completed correctly. Also, check with your attorney to be sure the designation works in conjunction with your estate plan.

Divorcee Double-Take

If you're divorced or going through a divorce, make sure you do a quick double check of your beneficiary designations. An ex-husband is usually prohibited by law from receiving anything under a Will written when you were still married. If, however, your former groom is still the beneficiary of an old life insurance policy, he'll likely receive the proceeds. Make sure the beneficiaries you want are named, not your ex.

We all know what life insurance is. Many of us have group term life insurance policies through our jobs. Others have policies, both term and whole life, that they've purchased in case of an early death. Life insurance proceeds are not taxable to your beneficiary. However, if you own and control a life insurance policy, the face value of the policy proceeds is included in your estate for estate tax purposes. What this means is that the full value of a million dollar life insurance policy will be included in your estate for estate tax purposes even though the policy is paid to your beneficiary. This is a big asset that you need to consider when creating your estate plan. More options for life insurance are discussed in Chapter 7, "What If You Want to Get Fancy with Your Planning?"

You're Worth It Statement

We all know you're worth it! Your lawyer will really know you're worth it if you come to your estate planning meeting with a detailed Net Worth Statement. Include how your property is owned and if there is a beneficiary designation for each asset. Here's what your statement should include:

NET WORTH STATEMENT

Asset	Ownership/ Beneficiary Designation	Current Value
Real Property		
Main Residence		
Vacation Home		
Time Share		
Business/Rental Property		
Vacant or Farm Land		
Other		
Personal Property		
Jewelry		
Antiques		
Sterling Silver		
Collections		
Artwork		
Equipment		
Automobiles		

Asset	Ownership/ Beneficiary Designation	Current Value
Personal Property		
Boats		
Motor homes		
Other		
Intangible Personal Property		
Stock		
Bonds		
Brokerage Accounts		
Bank Accounts		
Certificates of Deposit		
Annuities		
Business Interests		
Partnerships		
Patents		
Copyrights		
Stock Options		
Other Employee Benefit Items		
Property You Can Control (Trust Information) Include the names of any Trusts of which you are a beneficiary. If you have a copy of the Trust Agreement or Trust terms, attach a copy to your Net Worth Statement.		

Asset	Ownership/ Beneficiary Designation	Current Value
Assets with a Beneficiary Designation		
Individual Retirement Accounts		
401(k) or 403(b) Accounts		
Other Retirement Benefits		
Payable on Death Accounts		
Savings Bonds with a beneficiary designation		
Life Insurance—Include the face value of each life insurance policy as well as the cash surrender value, if any. Also note who owns the policy.		
Potential Inheritances Make a list of potential inheritances. Your attorney will understand that this is simply a guess on your part, but any estimate may help evaluate your estate planning options for these and your other assets.		
Liabilities		
Mortgage Debt		
Home Equity Line of Credit Debt		
Credit Card Debt		
Other Debt or Liabilities		

You probably noted that on the net worth list above I've included a provision for any assets you might inherit. By now you know that an inheritance is never an entitlement; but, if you think you might receive some significant assets from a parent or other relative, let your attorney know. Why? You may want to think about implementing some special planning for those assets. For example, one client hopes to segregate the assets she receives from her grandmother into a special Trust for her children's education, instead of giving her husband access to the funds. It's not that she doesn't want her husband to benefit; she just believes that this is in keeping with her family's tradition of providing for education first and foremost.

Everyday Estate Planning

No, you don't have to worry about your estate planning every day. But a big part of putting your affairs in order means, well, putting your affairs in order. Getting organized makes almost everyone's New Year's resolutions top 10 list. It certainly isn't easy, but you and your family will benefit from a little less clutter and a lot more orderliness. (I'll admit that I'd be able to fit in an extra 20 minutes of exercise every day with the time I've wasted looking for things—some of which I still can't find!)

Get Organized!

Make a list of all your bank accounts. Close old pass-book accounts and add them to your savings account. If you bank online, include your passwords (or a password hint) with your list of accounts. If you have more than two bank accounts—*consolidate*. No one needs accounts at a half dozen different institutions. It will save you from running from Bank A to Bank B. Plus, the FDIC insures deposits up to $100,000 at a single institution. Of course, if you have more than that, banking at different institutions is a good idea. Get rid of your old paper stock certificates. Paper gets lost—and it's really tough to transfer such shares upon death. Today, shares of stock are held as *book-entry* shares. In fact, you have to make a special request to receive an actual certificate. If you don't have a brokerage account, open one and have your certificated shares transferred into the account. Review all your beneficiary designations and keep them in an easy-to-find file for future reference. Prepare a detailed Letter of Instruction for your loved ones (see Chapter 9, "Is There Anything Else You Should Do to Be Prepared?"). You'll benefit from knowing where things are at a moment's notice—so will your beneficiaries.

Not being organized can cost you now with lost or escheated assets. It will definitely cost your loved ones after you pass. Why? They'll have to spend countless hours trying to reconstruct your finances and tracking down bank accounts and other assets. Alternatively, they'll have to hire professionals to assist them in sorting through box upon box of ancient paperwork. Worst of all, assets may remain undiscovered only to escheat to your state.

Unclaimed Property

If you have access to the Internet, do a quick search for unclaimed property that may have been turned over to your local state government. Check your state's Web site for more details. I've found everything from old dividend checks, to tax refunds, to ancient bank accounts for both family and clients. It only takes a few minutes—and the results might just surprise you!

Now that you know what your estate is comprised of, it's time to think about what that means for taxes and planning. Keep reading and you'll learn what you can do to make sure you meet your estate planning goals and how you can save, save, save on taxes.

What Should You Do Next?

1. Learn and understand how your assets are owned.

2. Complete your "You're Worth It Statement."

3. Organize your finances!

Chapter 3

Is It Really *That* Important to Think About Taxes?

As our founding father, Benjamin Franklin, wisely noted, the only certainties in life are death and taxes. What Mr. Franklin didn't realize at the time is that so many taxes would be associated with death. Elizabeth, age 68, agrees with our founding father: "The IRS shouldn't benefit after our demise; the government has already benefited throughout our working years." Taxes at your passing may be imposed by both the state and federal governments. We'll start with state inheritance tax.

Inheritance Tax

Many states have an inheritance tax. Generally, the amount of tax imposed is dependent on who receives the assets from your estate. In New Jersey, for example, there is no inheritance tax on assets received by spouses, descendants, ancestors, and charities. Pennsylvania imposes an inheritance tax on all individuals, except spouses, for inheritances over a certain amount. Each state is different. Check the Web site for your state's tax-ing authority to learn more.

Who Pays The Tax?

That's up to you! As part of your estate planning, dis-cuss with your attorney the options for tax payments. Many individuals prefer to have all taxes paid by their estates. Others prefer that the taxes be paid on a pro rata basis (each beneficiary paying his or her share of the tax based on what he or she received). In making this decision, it's important to think about assets that pass outside your Will (IRAs and life insurance, for instance) and the type of asset you are leaving some-one. Ask yourself: Is it something that's easy to sell to pay any taxes? Consider this example. You leave your estate in unequal shares: let's say 70 percent to Nicholas Nephew and 10 percent to each of Nancy Niece, Nina Niece, and Nora Niece. If all of the tax is paid by your estate, each of your nieces is paying a large portion of the tax imposed on the disposition to your nephew because their final distribution is reduced by the taxes paid on his share.

Generally, there's not much you can do to avoid the state inheritance tax; however, talk to your attorney. He or she may have some ideas to reduce the inheritance tax due on your passing. For example, in New Jersey, inheritance tax is imposed on siblings for transfers over $25,000; so many individuals limit the transfer to a sib-ling to this amount to avoid any inheritance tax.

Federal Estate Tax

In 2008, you're required to file a federal estate tax return for estates that have a gross value greater than $2,000,000. Many of you may be thinking, there's no way I need to worry about this tax or this return. If you did your homework and completed the "You're Worth It Statement" in Chapter 2, "What Exactly Does Your Estate Include?" you probably have a good idea as to the current value of your estate. For the rest of you, this is a not so subtle hint to go back and complete your Net Worth Statement. Why? Most of us can't believe we have as many assets as we do. In part, it's because we don't spend a lot of time counting our pennies. For others, you may not have realized that assets like life insurance, the home you own, and your 401(k) are counted as assets when determining if you must file a federal estate tax return.

The Taxing Tax Laws

If your estate exceeds $2,000,000 in 2008, your estate is required to file a federal estate tax return (IRS Form 706). In 2009, this amount increases to $3,500,000. If Congress doesn't make a change, there will be no estate tax in 2010, and the filing threshold will drop back to $1,000,000 in 2011 and thereafter. What happens next is anyone's guess...although most individuals practicing in this field believe there will be some change before 2010, which will likely result in changes in state laws as well. So how can you plan? Talk to your attorney. There are many plans that consider possible changes and provide flexibility to you and your loved ones.

So far, we've only discussed who needs to file a return. Now let's talk about whether or not a tax will be imposed. In simple terms, if your **gross estate** (the total value of your assets), less deductions, is greater than $2,000,000, federal estate tax is imposed. There are deductions for gifts to charity, any debts you owe at the time of your death (including mortgage debt), funeral expenses, and medical expenses. There is also an unlimited deduction for transfers made to or on behalf of your husband at your death.

If your estate is still over $2,000,000 in 2008, after your deductions, the highest federal estate tax rate that may be imposed is 45 percent. Yes, you read that right, under current tax laws as much as *45 percent* of your estate in excess of $2,000,000 may have to be paid to Uncle Sam. Here's a quick example. Dora Decedent has an estate valued at $3,500,000. She has $500,000 of deductions for expenses and gifts left to charity. The balance of her estate is paid to her two children. The approximate federal estate tax will be $450,000. So instead of receiving $1,500,000 each, each child will receive $1,275,000. While it's still an incredibly wonderful bequest, most individuals would rather see that extra $450,000 pass to their kids, not the IRS. Is there anything you can do to reduce the amount of your federal estate tax? Absolutely. There are many examples and suggestions in Chapters 6 ("What's a Will? What's a Trust? How Do You Use Them to Put Your Plan in Place?") and 7 ("What If You Want to Get Fancy with Your Planning?"). So keep reading!

State Estate Tax

Each state is different. Some impose inheritance taxes; some don't. The same is true of state estate taxes. Each state is different, not only in whether it imposes estate taxes, but also in how these taxes are calculated. Prior to 2001, your federal estate tax was reduced by the state death tax credit. In other words, the amount you paid to your state was directly linked, or coupled with, the tax paid to the federal government. Depending on where you lived, the state death tax credit was paid to your state. If there was no tax in your state, there was no credit. The state death tax credit, in effect, was a form of revenue sharing between the federal government and states. Beginning in 2001, the federal government phased out this credit. This left many states with a big revenue loss and resulted in some states imposing new rules and regulations for calculating their state's estate tax.

Several states took action and decoupled from the federal tax calculation, imposing their own tax structure. New Jersey, for example, now imposes New Jersey estate tax as if the decedent had died in 2001. So, for New Jersey estate tax purposes, the exclusion from estate tax is $675,000, even though the federal exclusion in 2008 is $2,000,000. Other states remain coupled with the federal tax system and only impose tax on estates that exceed the federal exclusion amount. This has created many planning challenges for women across the Garden and similar states. I'm the first to admit that this is horribly complicated. Talk to your attorney to understand what's what in your state.

In real terms, what does all this mean? It means it's important to consider all taxes when you talk to your attorney about the estate plan that's right for you. If you're married and your estate is large, you may want some state taxes to be paid when you die to shelter more money from Uncle Sam. But maybe not. Your circumstances are unique, and you need to consider all taxes when you're creating the plan that protects your assets.

Gift Tax

I love birthdays and holidays. And I love gifts! No, Uncle Sam doesn't impose a tax on that Christmas sweater or Hanukkah scarf; however, he does impose a tax on gifts valued in excess of $12,000. This is the current annual exclusion from gift tax. This exclusion amount is indexed annually for inflation and may change from one year to the next. In other words, you may make gifts of $12,000 to as many people as you would like in any given calendar year. You may also make unlimited gifts to your husband and to charities. The benefit of gifting is twofold. First, you can share your good fortune with others today.

Let's All Join In!

If your husband joins you in making gifts, you can increase the amount of your annual exclusion gift to $24,000. It's easy for him and terrific for your beneficiaries! Check with your tax preparer to see if you'll need to file gift tax returns.

Second, you can reduce the size of your estate for federal estate tax purposes. Here's a quick lesson in how gifting can help to reduce that tax burden. Judy has five children and ten grandchildren. Each year she makes an annual exclusion gift to each individual. Her total annual gifts are $180,000. If she continues to make annual exclusion gifts for five years, she will have reduced her estate by $900,000. That's a federal tax savings of as much as $405,000. Just a little something to think about!

Gifts, Gifts, and More Gifts!

In addition to annual exclusion gifts, you may make unlimited tuition and medical payments for anyone of your choosing. That's right: You can pay your grandson's grad school tuition or your neighbor's neurologist. The catch is that the payment must be made directly to the educational institution or health care provider and not to your friend or family member.

Gifts can be in cash, securities, personal property, or real estate. One consideration, though, is that when you give a gift of something other than cash, the recipient of the gift takes the gift at your cost basis (the value of the property when you bought, inherited, earned, or otherwise received it). Let's say you paid $10 a share for ABC Corporation. On the date of the gift, a share of ABC Corporation is worth $100 a share. If you give your daughter 10 shares of ABC Corporation, the value of the gift is $1,000. Your daughter's cost basis in the 10 shares is $100. If she sells the shares on the day she receives them, she will have a taxable capital gain of $900. Under current law, the capital gain tax rate is between 5% and 28% depending upon your income level and how long you've owned the asset you are selling. When you receive an asset as a gift, you take the basis of the person who gave you the asset, but you also take their carrying period. If your benefactor owned a security for years, you're treated as owning it for the same length of time. When you're deciding what gifts to give, you may want to consider potential capital gains.

Maybe you're super generous and are thinking, "If the tax savings are this great, why don't I just give it all away?" Well, the IRS knows that you generous gals are out there and has imposed limitations on what you can give away during your lifetime. Any gift in excess of the $12,000 annual exclusion from gift tax to a single person is considered a taxable gift. That, however, doesn't mean that you have to shell out a tax payment if a gift is $12,001. Instead, each dollar over $12,000 uses part of your lifetime applicable exclusion from gift tax. Currently, each individual's lifetime applicable exclusion from gift tax is $1,000,000. This means that during your lifetime, you can give away up to a total of $1,000,000 over your annual exclusion gifts without any gift tax being imposed. When your total gifts exceed $1,000,000, gift tax is imposed at a tax rate of up to 50 percent. Under current law, this rate will be reduced to 35 percent in 2010. Some states also impose a gift tax. Check with your attorney or accountant for details on your state's gift taxes.

Do you remember watching the Partridge Family? Well, what you didn't know is that Shirley Partridge hit it big as a solo artist after the show went off the air. As a result of her success, she decided to make gifts of $250,000 to each of her children: Keith, Laurie, Danny, Chris, and Tracy. Shirley generously wrote checks to each child on January 1, 2007. Because Shirley never did marry the band's manager, he couldn't join in the gifts. The result was a taxable gift in the amount of $238,000 being made to each child ($250,000 less the $12,000 annual gift tax exclusion). Shirley therefore made total gifts of $1,190,000 in 2007, which used up her entire lifetime exclusion from gift tax. Her gifts resulted in a $190,000 taxable gift that generated a gift tax of about $85,000. I don't think I love that!

For each dollar of your lifetime applicable exclusion from gift tax you use, you reduce the amount you may pass tax free upon your death. In other words, if you made taxable gifts of $500,000 in January 2008, and died later that year, your estate would only have $1,500,000 left of your exclusion from estate tax to apply to your estate. So, why make such big gifts? As noted above, you may want to help your loved ones today. However, big gifts are also helpful to remove appreciable assets from your estate. Look at it this way. If you give $500,000 to your granddaughter, you no longer have that money. It can't earn income and it can't grow. If you live 10 years after making the gift, you've really given away $815,000 (the initial $500,000 gift plus 10 years of 5 percent returns). That's more than a 50 percent added benefit to your gift—and that's not bad.

For a gift to qualify for the annual exclusion from gift tax, the gift must be a present interest gift. In other words, the recipient of the gift must be able to use the gift when the gift is made. A gift that takes effect in the future isn't a present interest gift and won't be considered an annual exclusion gift. For example, if you put $12,000 in a Trust for your son, but he has no right to use the funds for five years, it's not an annual exclusion gift. To qualify some transfers as present interest gifts, beneficiaries may be given a right to withdraw the contributed funds. This is referred to as a Crummey power.

A note of caution: A gift is just that, a gift. You're giving something up without any compensation. If you make a gift, you cannot expect that the recipient will return the gift if you need it in the future. As much as you might like to, you cannot attach strings to your gifts. You must be comfortable with parting with your assets if you're going to begin or continue making gifts. Believe me, there are many very wealthy individuals who aren't comfortable giving up their assets, despite some very beneficial tax results. While I'll continue to encourage you to think about it, this is something you should consider only if it works for you.

Giving gifts is not only fun, but it can also provide some real tax benefits for your estate. There are many people who would love to engage in regular gifting but don't have the liquidity to do so. Luckily there are other options available. Jump ahead to Chapter 7 to learn more about gifting opportunities.

Generation Skipping Transfer Tax

I deal with taxes every day. Hands down, the most complicated tax is the **generation skipping transfer tax**. In simple terms, this is a tax imposed when you skip a generation in making gifts or leaving a bequest. If you decide that your Wall Street whiz son doesn't need your hard-earned estate, you can skip over him and leave your estate directly to your grandchildren. However, if the amount you leave your grandchildren exceeds $2,000,000 (the 2008 exclusion from the generation skipping transfer tax), generation skipping transfer tax is imposed, in addition to the regular estate tax, at a rate of 50 percent. For this reason, it's wise to consult with a lawyer before you decide to pass over your kids for the next generation. At the very least, limit generation skipping transfers to the amount of the allowable exclusion ($2,000,000 in 2008).

If You Don't Fly First Class, Your Children Will

No, you don't have to fly first class. But you shouldn't be afraid to spend a little money on yourself either. If you have a taxable estate, your estate may pay tax at rates as great as 45 percent. The way I look at it, for every dollar you have over the tax threshold, you're really only spending 55 cents of every dollar on yourself when you book a first class plane ticket. Your kids may not like the advice—but it's your money, so enjoy it!

Income Tax

Believe it or not, income tax doesn't end when you've died. That's right, the income your estate earns after you die (this can be interest and dividends, for example) is taxed just like it was taxed when you were alive. Your estate files income tax returns similar to those annoying forms you've always filed, it's just a different form (Form 1041). Your estate files a similar form for state purposes as well. Unfortunately, there's no way to avoid this tax. It's just something to be aware of.

Taxing, isn't it—all this talk of tax? There isn't much we can do about many of these taxes, but there *is* a lot we can do to reduce state and federal estate taxes. If it takes the idea of paying more in tax to inspire you to do some estate planning, great! I've done my job. Read more in Chapters 6 and 7 on how to implement tax savings planning in both straightforward and complicated ways. The choice is yours, but I know my choice is saving tax dollars!

What Should You Do Next?

1. Learn what taxes may apply to your estate.
2. Decide how your beneficiaries should pay the tax.
3. Consider the benefits of gift-giving.
4. Spend a little on yourself!

Chapter 4

Who Makes Sure Everything You Want to Have Happen Happens When You're Gone?

Whether we admit it or not, death will happen. The only question is *when*. That's why it's important to decide today who will manage your affairs when you've passed on. While the choice may seem obvious, it's worth some careful and thoughtful consideration.

Your **fiduciary**, whether it's a bank, trust company, or individual Executor, Trustee, or Guardian, has a duty to exercise care and responsibility. In legal circles, we refer to this as a **fiduciary duty** to act with trust and good faith. To avoid additional costs to your estate, be sure that your Will contains a statement that no surety bond (a kind of insurance policy) will be required of any of your fiduciaries. When you're selecting your fiduciaries, don't limit your decision to just one person. Always name one, two, or more successors to ensure your estate is being handled by those you intend in the event your first choices can't serve.

Fiduciary First Team

Administrator—The individual or financial institution appointed to oversee the estate of a person dying without a valid Will or if no Executor or Personal Representative has been named. A female administrator is also referred to as an *Administratrix*.

Conservator—The individual appointed by a court to manage the financial affairs of an incapacitated person.

Executor or Personal Representative—The individual or financial institution that carries out the provisions of a Will. A female Executor is also referred to as an *Executrix*.

Fiduciary—The individual or financial institution acting for the benefit of an estate, Trust, or person and includes an *Executor, Trustee, Guardian, Conservator*, and *Administrator*.

Guardian—The individual granted the power to take care of the person and property of a minor or incapacitated person.

Trustee—The individual or financial institution that administers a Trust.

Guardians

The number one concern of mothers everywhere is, "Who will care for my children if I die while they're still minors?" If there is one reason—and one reason alone—why you should put an estate plan into place, it's to name a Guardian to care for your minor children. A Guardian can only be named in your Will. But how do you choose a Guardian? Focus on the individual who will love your offspring and raise them as you would. Don't worry about who can afford more mouths to feed or who lives in your community. Instead, follow your gut instinct and select the friend or family member who will treat your children as their own and share with them the beliefs and values you cherish.

There are other considerations. You love your brother, but his choice of wife is, shall we say, less than desirable. Or, maybe your best friend would be perfect, but she has five children of her own and is battling breast cancer. Think twice before naming a married couple. Instead name your sister if she's your top choice; it makes it easier if she and your brother-in-law divorce in the future. Alternatively, make it clear in your Will that if your sister and brother-in-law call it quits, your sister becomes the sole Guardian.

The excuse I hear most often from couples pro-crastinating in completing their estate planning is, "We can't decide on a Guardian." Remember that your Will can be changed at any time as long as you still have the capacity to sign a Will. Select the best person right now, instead of agonizing over the decision and doing noth-ing. Missy, age 38, agrees, "Pick or don't pick, but get the estate planning done!" It's much better to have a Guardian named than to have no estate plan in place if the worst happens. If you don't say what you want, your families could fight over Guardianship. The end result is that the Court may decide who steps in as Guardian. Nothing against Judge Judy and her colleagues, but that's the last thing I'd want. And, of course, don't stop at just one Guardian. You should always have two suc-cessor Guardians because the person you name might be unable to act or may also have passed away. If your choice of Guardian changes in the future, modify your Will with a simple Codicil.

Doesn't a Godparent Serve as Guardian?

The godparents you lovingly selected for your newborn have the duty, depending on your religion, to sponsor a child at baptism and to take a role in your little one's religious education. It's a big job, but that's where it ends. Godparents do not become a child's Guardian if you die unless you specifically name them in your Will to serve as Guardians.

If you really can't decide, consider co-Guardians. Pick one person to have primary custody, but another to assist in all major life decisions (such as education, medical treatment, and development) for your children. Be creative. Talk to your attorney. You may find a solution that works best for your circumstances and concerns.

You may also differentiate between guardian of the person and guardian of the property. A **guardian of the person** takes care of your children's welfare and custody. A **guardian of the property** takes care of your tiny tot's assets. Most folks don't differentiate between these roles, instead naming a Trustee to care for the funds they leave their loved ones. However, using two different Guardians might just work for you.

Guardians aren't limited to your wee ones. There are many parents serving as court-appointed Guardians for their disabled adult children. If you're currently serving as a court-appointed Guardian for a child, or any other individual for that matter, some states allow you to name a successor court-appointed Guardian to succeed you on your passing. Be sure to tell your attorney if you're serving for anyone in this capacity.

Many individuals include directions in their Wills discussing their hopes, dreams, and goals for their children. Some requests are very specific: requiring visitation with certain relatives, expecting frequent travel to favorite locations, or encouraging particular educational opportunities. Others are more general desires: that a Guardian attend to the child's needs, consider the child's likes, and keep the child safe from harm. Often, a mother will write a Letter of Guidance to help the person she named as Guardian in the unthinkable task of raising her family.

Letter of Guidance for Guardians

Every year, I spend a long weekend with my closest friends from college and watch their parenting skills in action. My friends are all terrific mothers, each one with her own unique priorities, passions, dreams, and hopes for her brood. That's why I continually encourage them to put their feelings in writing in a Letter of Guidance for their named Guardians. These letters might state whether religious education is important, as well as views on primary, secondary, and college education. Providing direction to the person who might raise your child shouldn't be limited to traditional issues. Note your views on music, camp, foreign language, sports, travel, dating, allowances, and anything else that you feel passionately about. Your Guardians won't know how you feel unless you tell them—and writing it down is a great way to get your message across.

Executors

Your **Executor** or **Personal Representative** is the person or financial institution that administers your estate. In other words, your Executor is in charge of everything related to your estate after you die. That means arranging your funeral (if you haven't already done that—see Chapter 9, "Is There Anything Else You Should Do to Be Prepared?"), paying your bills and any taxes, figuring out what your assets are, selling assets if necessary (and that means cleaning out that dirty attic and holding a garage sale for you packrats!) and then distributing your estate as you've requested in your Last Will and Testament. Generally, it's a job that lasts for a few years. The difficulty of the job depends on the complexity of your estate and your estate plan, your assets, and your beneficiaries. If you have 92 beneficiaries, the job will be much more difficult than if you have two beneficiaries. While it shouldn't be a factor, the ability of your Executor and beneficiaries to get along is also important. If there is friction or animosity, your Executor's job is much more difficult.

Deciding who should serve as Executor can be difficult. If you're married, your husband may be the logical choice. But if it's your second or third husband and your children are all from your first marriage, well, maybe the obvious choice is no longer the best choice. When deciding who to select, the best advice I can give my clients is to select the individual who is smart enough to ask for help. You don't need a financial whiz kid or the only lawyer in the family. Instead, you should select the person who understands your goals, understands his or her responsibility, and can fulfill all obligations and duties. Often, legal fights over estates have nothing to do with the Will, but instead focus on the Executor who just isn't getting the job done, isn't communicating, and is trying to benefit him- or herself above the other beneficiaries.

Does Your Executor Get Paid?

Most state laws dictate how much an Executor is paid (although an Executor doesn't have to accept payment). Usually, there are both income and corpus commissions. Income commissions are based on the income earned by an estate. Corpus commissions are based on the value of the assets that are distributed according to your Will. There are usually no corpus commissions on joint tenancy assets or assets with a beneficiary designation. You can also enter into a separate agreement outlining how your Executor will be paid. If you're naming a bank or Trust company, ask for a copy of its current fee schedule to be sure you are satisfied with its charges.

If your loved ones just can't get along, consider a Corporate Executor. This is a bank or trust company with authority to act as an Executor or Personal Representative. These professionals are efficient and effective in administering estates. They know what they're doing and will get the job done. If you have a particularly difficult beneficiary (such as a mentally disabled individual or a child with a chip on his or her shoulder the size of the Rock of Gibraltar), a corporate fiduciary can take the burden off your other loved ones and prevent further family disputes. Many corporate fiduciaries may have minimum estates that they work with; however, smaller, regional institutions will often have services available regardless of your estate's size. If you're interested in a corporate fiduciary, interview local banks and Trust companies to find the fit that is best for your family.

What If the Person You've Named Can't Do the Job?

That's what successors are for! We can't anticipate the future for ourselves or for anyone else. Your sister might be the perfect candidate to serve as your Executor today; but in ten years she might be ill and unable to serve. Remember, no one ever has to act and may renounce his or her appointment. So don't think that by naming someone you've sentenced them to a job they can't get out of—they can always step down from the appointment you've made.

Sometimes the best solution is to have more than one individual serve as Executor or to appoint an individual to serve along with a Corporate Executor. When considering naming more than one Executor, consider whether the parties can act together. If you have two children who spend all their time fighting, it's probably best not to name them as co-Executors. Also, the more people you name, the harder it can be to coordinate efforts. For example, if you have three Executors and all three have to sign contracts and Deeds, it can slow down the process of handling your estate. On the other hand, it can be beneficial to have the responsibility shared among several individuals. It takes the pressure off each individual and allows each person to take on the tasks that he or she is good at. If you name more than one individual, you can include a provision in your Will that your Executors are to act unanimously or in concert with the majority.

If you don't have a Will and don't name an Executor, the individual who serves on your behalf is a court-appointed **Administrator** or **Personal Representative**. An Administrator could also be appointed by a court if all of the individuals you named as Executor are unable to or refuse to act. Again, because it bears repeating, that's why naming successors is so important.

Trustees

Many of us want to care for our loved ones by providing that funds for their benefit be held in Trust. There are many types of Trusts, which are discussed at length in Chapters 6 and 7 ("What's a Will? What's a Trust? How Do You Use Them to Put Your Plan in Place?" and "What If You Want to Get Fancy with Your Planning?" respectively). Maybe the Trust you select will last for just a few years. Or, maybe a Trust will last until a certain age or ages for your young children. For other beneficiaries, the funds may be held in Trust for their lifetime. The **Trustee** is the person or institution you identify to manage those funds during the length of the

Trust. Like your Executor and Guardian, your Trustee has a fiduciary duty to manage the funds with trust and good faith.

Your Trustee also has a duty to weigh the interests of both the **lifetime beneficiary** and the **remainder beneficiary**. The lifetime, or income, beneficiary is the beneficiary who has a current interest in either or both the income and principal of the Trust. For example, a Trust you establish for your husband may provide him with all of the Trust income, plus principal, as needed for his health, support, and maintenance during his lifetime, in the Trustee's discretion. The Trustee, therefore, in making investment and other decisions, must weigh the needs of your husband against the future beneficiaries who receive the Trust assets at your husband's death. These future beneficiaries of the Trust are the remainder beneficiaries. While serving as Trustee is usually a straight-forward job, it can be difficult if the income and remainder beneficiaries don't get along or have different objectives. For example, the income beneficiary requests that the Trust assets be invested in high-income securities, while the remainder beneficiaries want high-growth investments. Also, depending upon the age of your beneficiaries, the job of a Trustee can last for decades.

It's for these reasons that the selection of your Trustee is so important. Like your Executor, your Trustee can be a person or a financial institution. You don't have to select a financial genius, but you should select someone who can ask for help from an attorney and financial planner. You also want to select someone who understands the needs of your Trust beneficiaries and will act in their best interests. You can have one, two, or more Trustees. They can be a combination of people or individuals and a corporate fiduciary. Again, selecting successor Trustees is incredibly important, especially for Trusts that can go on for what seems like forever.

For both your Executors and Trustees, it is wise to provide for the ability to name successor or replacement fiduciaries. If an individual currently serving is the last named Trustee, you want him or her to be able to select a replacement, perhaps from the next generation. It's also important for the currently serving individual Trustee or the beneficiaries to appoint a replacement corporate fiduciary. As was noted earlier, financial institutions are merging so quickly we can barely remember where we bank. You want your beneficiaries to be able to switch corporate fiduciaries if the new entity no longer provides the personal attention they deserve—or has an investment philosophy that is unsatisfactory to the individual Trustee or beneficiaries.

Identifying the people or institutions to act on your behalf isn't easy. But not selecting someone is far worse. Remember, unless a Trust you establish is irrevocable or you lose your capacity to execute your estate planning documents, you can always change your selection. Isn't making a decision better than having a court make the decision for you or having your family waging war to determine who should act? Don't let your inability to decide these important roles keep you from putting your plan in place. It's simply inexcusable.

What Should You Do Next?

1. Identify Guardians for your minor and disabled children.
2. Write a Letter of Guidance for your Guardians.
3. Select an Executor and successor Executors.
4. Choose a Trustee and successor Trustees.

Chapter 5

What Will Happen to Your Loved Ones?

For most of us, our number one objective is to care for our loved ones. The goals of young-at-heart Jane probably reflect most of our hopes: "...That all our family shares our assets with no acrimony or ill will—that our family enjoys our good fortune—that our estate helps those who need help and continues to grow for those that have the ability to invest for the next generation." Stephanie, age 42, feels the same way: "I hope I don't leave a mess for my survivors to deal with. I hope I am remembered fondly, my assets are disbursed according to my wishes, and my family keeps only the things of mine that have meaning and happy memories associated with them." I couldn't have said it better myself!

Your loved ones can be anyone (that's what's so wonderful about the expression!). It acknowledges that those we love aren't necessarily our families, but our friends as well. For others, our loved ones are four-legged friends or favorite charities. The beauty of creating your own estate plan is that you have the ability to choose just who receives your bounty. Who you provide for—and how you provide for them—is your call. As I always say to my clients, "I don't care who you pick, as long as you pick who you want!"

Wills of the Who's Who

Even the rich and famous have to sign Wills. Here's a sneak peek at some of the loved ones these *People* magazine cover girls took care of in their Wills:

Jacqueline Kennedy Onassis established Trusts of $500,000 for each of her sister's (Lee B. Radziwill) children. She gave her Martha's Vineyard retreat, and other real estate, to her children. The residue of her estate was used to establish a charitable Trust called The J Foundation.

Diana, Princess of Wales created a Trust for her sons, Prince William and Prince Harry, to be distributed to them when they turn 25.

Vickie Lynn Marshall (a/k/a Anna Nicole Smith) wrote a Will that only provided for her son, Daniel, who died before she did. There was no provision for her daughter, Dannielynn. In fact her Will specifically stated that no other children receive benefits from her estate (the perfect example of terrible planning).

Marilyn Monroe created a Trust for her mother that paid her $5,000 each year.

Husbands

He's your soul mate, your better half, or maybe your ball and chain. Whether he's in the dog house or not, he's your main man. And, if you're like most women, he's your number one priority. You want to (and do!) take care of him. Taking care of him includes providing for him on your death. In fact, spouses are so important in the United States that anything you leave your American husband qualifies for the unlimited marital deduction from federal estate tax. That doesn't, however, mean leaving him everything is the way to go. Chapter 6 ("What's a Will? What's a Trust? How Do You Use Them to Put Your Plan in Place?") will explain more. There are also many ways for you and Mr. Right to work together as a couple to minimize taxes on both of your deaths. Think about what's right for your husband and your family when you're deciding what estate plan works for you. Unless you've signed a pre- or antenuptial agreement, your life partner is also your responsibility. He may have more money (and better hair) than Donald Trump, but he's still entitled to a share of your estate. You'll learn about that in Chapter 6 as well.

Significant Others

Walking down the aisle isn't for everyone. That's why we've come up with so many wonderful expressions to describe our significant other: partner, companion, mate, other half. You may not have tied the knot, but your relationship is just as solid and committed. This is the person you want to take care of when you're no longer here.

Even if you've cohabited for decades, the laws of intestacy rarely protect your "roommate." There are a handful of states that recognize common law marriage; check with your lawyer to see if this applies to your relationship. Some states recognize your partner as your spouse if you're gay, but only if you've registered as such. If you're in a committed relationship but unmarried, you must, must, must have a Will or Trust to make it clear that your loved one gets your property. Except in rare circumstances, the law will not protect your better half if you aren't married. Period. And, except in some states, your companion is taxed just like a friend. For inheritance tax purposes, this is often the highest tax rate. There's also no available marital deduction for federal tax purposes. Planning in this situation is incredibly important.

The options available to care for your significant other are vast. There are Trusts for life or for a term of years; distributions can be outright; or, maybe you'll establish a charitable Trust that provides your lover an income stream for life, with the principal used for charitable purposes on his or her death. What you decide is up to you—it's just important to decide something.

Children

If you're a mother, I bet you spend every single waking hour (and probably some sleepless nights as well!) thinking about your kids, whether they're 2, 22, or 42. You want to be sure they'll be okay when you die. The only difference is how they'll be okay. When your little ones are babies, tweens, and teenagers, you worry about who will take care of them if the unthinkable happens. Who will raise them? How will college be paid for? For moms with adult children, your concerns change to how well they'll handle your death, the paperwork, and everything that needs to be done.

In Chapters 6 and 7, "What If You Want to Get Fancy with Your Planning?" you'll learn more about planning for your kids. In addition to Wills and Trusts, there are other ideas to help you give some of your estate away today. **Section 529 plans** are state authorized education savings plans. These plans allow funds contributed to the plan to grow tax-free. If the proceeds are used to pay for college, no federal income tax will ever be imposed. States don't tax the money until it's used. Additionally, if the funds aren't used for education, there are penalties to pay when you withdraw them from the 529 account. Because they're state sponsored, investment choices may be limited.

Adopted Children and Sons and Daughters In-Law

Unless your estate planning documents state otherwise, legally adopted children are treated as natural children in most circumstances. If you don't want an adopted child to take a share of your estate, your Will must specifically state this. You can also limit adopted children to individuals adopted as minors (yes, there is such a thing as adult adoption). Your kids-in-law will not be beneficiaries of your estate or Trust unless you specifically provide for them. However, you have no control over what your son or daughter does with his or her inherited assets after you're gone! Hmmm...seems like a good reason to discuss estate planning with your married children.

You can also open up a **Uniform Transfers to Minors Act (UTMA)** or **Uniform Gifts to Minors Act (UGMA)** account for a child, grandchild, niece, nephew, or other youngster. A parent or other adult serves as custodian of the account. The money in the account can be invested in anything from bank deposits, bonds, stock, certificates of deposit, or other securities. There's no tax break with UTMA and UGMA accounts. Taxes must be paid every year, and in some situations the parent of the child (depending on the child's age and income) could be taxed on the income earned by these accounts. Because nothing is perfect, these accounts can be accessed (can you say spent?) by the beneficiary at the age of majority (18 in some states, 21 in others). Check with your financial planner for more details. If you're worried about contributing to an account that your little ones can access when they're still in school, there's another alternative. Establish a Trust today that provides for your kids or grandkids. You can use this Trust to hold your annual exclusion gifts. Turn ahead to Chapter 7 to learn more.

Because a lot of money in the hands of an 18 year old can be disastrous, you'll want your Will to provide that funds for your kids be held in Trust until certain ages (the same is true for grandchildren, nieces, and nephews). As you'll learn in Chapter 6, I believe that spreading distributions out over a period of time works very well, with distributions at ages 25, 30, and 35, for example.

Planning Party

Estate planning is a family plan. If your family is close, and everyone gets along, consider discussing your thoughts with your nearest and dearest. Why? They may have some interesting ideas. Or more importantly, they may share something with you that you didn't know. Maybe they haven't told you that your grandson has a mild disability and any money he receives from you could jeopardize his government benefits. You thought your daughter was doing well, but you learn that she's doing so well that it makes sense to skip her and leave her share of your estate to her children.

Missy's 95-year-old grandmother talked to her seven children before doing her estate planning and asked if they'd rather have their shares go directly to them or skip ahead to their children. Each child made the best decision for his or her family. Three opted for their inheritance to pass to grandchildren; while four requested their shares directly. For Missy, her grandmother's planning resulted in "her estate passing as she had planned, in a manner that held no surprises for anyone."

Singles often think that they'll just leave everything to their folks. Again, this is not necessarily the best idea. Why have assets taxed on your death go to your mom and dad to be taxed on their deaths?

A word of warning: If your family isn't close, fights all the time, or has competing interests (you have children from different marriages), don't bring the subject up, especially if you're thinking of treating your next of kin unequally.

So what about your older kids? Does that mean a Trust won't work? Absolutely not. At a certain age, you may think that your offspring can handle your money. I've had two clients in their 80s who visited my office because their mothers had just died. I'd guess, at that point, there was no worry about them being mature enough to handle an inheritance! But, maybe you're not so sure. Trusts can be established for spendthrift sons and drug-addicted daughters. Explain your concerns to your attorney so you can work together to craft a Trust that addresses your child's circumstances.

Not only is it important to think about how children will receive their inheritance, but also how much they'll receive. While most mothers want to treat their children equally, don't feel obligated to do so. As noted above, you may have a child who has been wildly successful who doesn't need any of your money. You may also have a child who has been a total disappointment, is in jail, or is...well...who knows where. Or maybe you have a disabled grandchild and you've decided that everything you have should be used to help him or her. In deciding how your loved ones benefit from your estate, if you feel strongly that one or more of your children not receive any benefit, exclude them. This is your decision. You have to do what's right for you and your entire family, not what you think you should do.

Disabled Loved Ones

If you don't have a disabled loved one, chances are someone you know does. Today, there are terrific benefits available to disabled individuals from the government, charities, and private organizations. These benefits aren't available to everyone. In many situations, if a disabled individual has money, he or she needs to spend his or her money first, before government and other benefits become available.

So, does that mean you just cut those who need your help the most out of your estate? Not at all! What it does mean is that you need to talk to an attorney knowledgeable in disability planning. He or she can counsel you on the benefits of Special Needs and Supplemental Benefits Trusts. These types of Trusts are drafted following specific government language. They can provide benefits to your loved ones that supplement government and other benefits. In other words, the funds in these Trusts can be used to pay for life's extras, such as a computer, an iPod, vacations, specially-equipped vehicles, and even a home that's handicapped accessible, without jeopardizing government benefits.

Grandchildren

If you're like my mom, you love your grandkids—and they love you back and then some. You can spoil them rotten (and you do!). You worry about them today, and you worry about their future. Like your other beneficiaries, there are many means to provide for descendants, now and in the future. Of course, as noted in Chapter 3 ("Is It Really *That* Important to Think About Taxes?"), what you can do is limited by the generation skipping transfer tax; so keep that in mind if you're considering really big gifts to a younger generation.

While you're alive, you can set up education or UTMA (Uniform Transfers to Minors Act) or UGMA (Uniform Gifts to Minors Act) accounts. You may make tuition payments and pay medical bills. When you die, you can provide for small bequests or set up Trusts. Again, the options are as unlimited as your little one's smiles!

Friends and Other Family

Your generosity needn't be limited to your branch of the family tree. It can extend to distant relatives and next-door neighbors. You can make gifts during life or at death (these are called **bequests** or **devises**). You can provide small tokens of friendship or large bequests in appreciation of decades of kindness. It doesn't matter that your beneficiary isn't an immediate family member. Your beneficiaries can, and should, be anyone you want them to be!

Pooches and Other Pets

Whether your best friend is Spot or Fluffy, you love your pet. Your four-legged pal is a member of the family and your most constant companion. That's why, for many, you're so concerned about your pet's well-being after you've died.

First and foremost, you're worried about who will care for your animal friend. Include a clause in your Will requesting that a certain individual adopt your pet. You can include a request that adoption expenses be paid by your estate or that the adoptive parent receive a small bequest in appreciation of his or her becoming Guardian. Can you leave money directly to Spot or Fluffy? No. But you can set up a Trust for your dog, cat, or other family friend. Talk to your counselor to learn more.

The Twelve Million Dollar Dog

The tabloid-proclaimed Queen of Mean, billionaire Leona Helmsley, left $12,000,000 in Trust for her best friend, her dog Trouble. Trouble will also be buried in the family mausoleum, next to Mrs. Helmsley. Wow, talk about a privileged pooch!

Charities

We've all spent time pitching in to help others, whether it was a Girl Scout food drive or cleaning up a park in college. Maybe you volunteer at your church or at a local school. There are organizations that tug at your heartstrings. You help in any way you can. Your dedication and loyalty don't need to end at death. Many women provide bequests in their Wills or Trusts—often a dollar amount devise to a religious organization, favorite school, or local charity. Others give everything to one or more nonprofit organizations. Your property can also be held in Trust for the benefit of your favorite entities. The options, as with all estate planning, are limitless.

Charity 411

The IRS Web site (www.irs.gov) provides a list of legitimate charities. Follow the Web site directions to learn if the charity you're considering is an authorized entity. If it's not, your estate will lose the charitable contribution for any bequests to this organization. Of course, the IRS would love to be your charity!

Charitable giving does more than make you feel warm and fuzzy. Gifts to qualified charities, both during life and at death, are tax deductible. Contributions while you're alive can qualify for an income deduction of up to 50 percent of your adjusted gross income. This amount may be reduced depending on your other deductions and income level. Check with your tax preparer. Donations made at death qualify for an estate tax deduction with no limit on their deductibility.

The news is full of exceptionally wealthy women providing for charities on their deaths (Brooke Astor and Leona Helmsley, for example). Yes, they're charitable. But they're also controlling. If you have an estate that is subject to significant tax, you can pay the tax and let your favorite uncle (Uncle Sam) decide where the money goes. Or, you can name the charities you want to receive your hard-earned money. Your choice versus Uncle Sam's choice—just a little something to think about. Charitable giving isn't for everyone—but for many, it's one of the wisest moves you can make.

There's so much you can do for your nearest and dearest, both now and in the future. Deciding who you want to benefit will be easy for some, and difficult for others. Think of your estate as a big pie. How many slices of pie are there? Who do you want to receive each piece? The slices don't need to be equal. Some can be big, and some can be small. Once you've decided the size of the pie slices, determine who receives what piece and the best ways to serve up those pie slices!

What Should You Do Next?

1. Identify the objects of your bounty—family members, friends, charities, or some combination of all three.

2. Consider talking to your loved ones about their plans to be sure your plans are complementary.

What's a Will? What's a Trust? How Do You Use Them to Put Your Plan in Place?

By now you know how to contact an attorney, and hopefully you already have an appointment scheduled. If not, you know what to do! You also have an idea as to the value of your estate and some idea as to your goals. The next item on your To Do list is to ask your lawyer to put pen to paper to prepare a Will and other testamentary documents that put your good intentions into action. You'll find basic estate planning concepts in this chapter, with more sophisticated and fancy planning in Chapter 7 ("What If You Want to Get Fancy with Your Planning?").

Last Wills and Testaments

Okay, we're friends by now, right? So we'll dispense with the formality and just call them *Wills*. Usually a formal document, a *Will* is, thanks to www. dictionary.com, a "legal declaration of a person's mind as to the manner in which she would have her property or estate disposed of after her death." Note that the definition says *legal declaration* not legal document. You don't need a lawyer to prepare your Will; but, as noted above, I strongly suggest it.

The Cocktail Napkin Will

We've all heard stories about the Will written on a cocktail napkin at a local watering hole. Believe it or not, this is a **holographic Will**. Written entirely in the handwriting of the person making the Will, a holographic Will is not witnessed or notarized. Whether a holographic Will is admissible in Court as a *real* Will depends on the state in which you reside.

As you're about to find out, Wills and other estate planning documents aren't simple forms. They're complex and detailed. They should be tailored to your particular needs, circumstances, and goals. Your Will can differ from your best friend's Will on everything from how taxes are paid to how your significant others are provided for, your assets distributed, and your kids cared for. Your Will is all about *you*; so don't use a form that's designed for just anyone. We all know that you're not just anyone!

Who's the Testatrix?

Even though it sounds like some unpleasant medication, a woman who leaves behind a valid Will at death is referred to as a Testatrix. In some states that no longer distinguish between men and women, you're referred to as a **Testator**.

Every Will should begin by stating that the Will you're signing is, in fact, your Will; you declare it to be your Will; and it revokes all other Wills you may have signed. Although the order of the following provisions may be different in each Will, every testamentary document should provide for the following. First, your Will should state that your estate will pay all of the expenses associated with your death. This would include the costs of your funeral, legal fees, and administration expenses such as postage, moving and storage costs, Executor's commissions, and court or probate fees. You also want your estate to pay your debts, including medical bills, credit card debt (and you were hoping to keep that secret!), past-due income taxes, and even your cell phone charges. Unless you specifically state otherwise, your debts do not include your mortgage or home equity line of credit, which remains with the mortgaged real estate. You should also outline who pays the taxes associated with your estate. Are they to be paid off the top before your property is divided up or on a pro rata basis by each beneficiary? Your attorney should be able to provide you with additional guidance in deciding what's best for your particular circumstances.

Who Can't Sign A Will?

Individuals under the age of 18 can't sign a Will because they don't have the legal capacity to enter into a contract. Incapacitated individuals are also unable to sign a Will because they aren't competent to make decisions, communicate their wishes, understand information, and evaluate choices and options.

Next, it's time to distribute your assets. Generally, tangible personal property (you know, everything you can touch and feel like cars, jewelry, sports equipment, paintings, knick-knacks, and furniture) is treated separately. Believe it or not, the biggest family disputes, arguments, and wars are often over your, well, stuff. That's why it's so important to take the time to think about everything from your antique armoire to your zebra-striped ottoman. In many states, you may leave a memorandum of your personal property to be treated as part of your Will. The memo should be in your own handwriting and provide detail not only about the item you're leaving, but also about who should receive that item. Again, be specific! Don't just say, "My gold necklace is for Goldie." Instead, your list should state, "My 18-inch gold serpentine necklace with the heart-shaped closure should be given to my girlfriend, Goldie Greatfriend." The more detail you provide, the fewer questions and the fewer opportunities for conflict. If you've already had an appraisal completed, use it as your guide, making notes directly on a copy of the appraisal. The personal property you include on your list shouldn't be limited to valuables. Include the items that are important to you that you want someone to have. Vanessa, age 39, wishes her grandmother had taken the time to make a list. Instead, Vanessa's aunt walked off with everything without providing Vanessa with a single remembrance of her grandmother, and all Vanessa wanted was an old, cracked teacup.

The benefit of using a list in addition to your Will is that it may be updated whenever your loved ones buy you more jewels. Feel free to read this to your husband—it is definitely a not so subtle hint. If you live in a state that does not permit the use of memorandums, include important items in your Will. Be sure that you include language in your Will stating that any disputes are to be resolved by your Executor or Personal Representative. Be careful. If you're going to the trouble of making a list, don't make oral promises also. Such promises will only lead to confusion, arguments, and heartbreak.

As for everything that isn't on your list (because who could possibly list everything they own!), consider leaving instructions for how items should be divided. You could ask your Executor or Personal Representative to make the decision. Or, instead, provide a plan for distribution. Include a request that only your beneficiaries be present as your property is being divided. Trouble starts when third parties toss out their two cents. Here are a few ideas:

1. **Draw numbers**—Each beneficiary draws a number. The beneficiary who picks number 1 picks an item of personal property. Then number two selects, then number three, and so on. After the highest number picks, number one selects again, and the selection circle continues until all wanted items have been chosen.

2. **Equal shares**—Ask that your personal property items be appraised. The total appraised value should be divided by the number of beneficiaries. For example, if the total appraised value is $18,000, and you have three beneficiaries, each may select items totaling $6,000 in value. Each beneficiary draws a number and selections are made in order of the numbers drawn. As soon as a beneficiary reaches his or her share of the appraised value, he or she cannot make any more selections.

3. **I wish I may, I wish I might**—Request that each beneficiary prepare a wish list of your personal property. Your Executor or Personal Representative should review and compare the lists. If only one person wants a particular item, it passes to the person who requested it. Items requested by more than one individual are divided by drawing numbers and selecting in order.

4. **It's better to give**—Direct that all items of value (artwork, antiques, jewelry, and collections) be donated to an appropriate museum or historical society. Clothing, personal items, furniture, and electronics may be donated to local or national charities.

5. **Going once, going twice**—Direct that all of your personal property be sold, especially if you're concerned that your beneficiaries will do nothing but fight. The proceeds of sale may be added to your other assets and distributed according to your Will.

In Chapter 3 ("Is It Really *That* Important to Think About Taxes?") we discussed the benefit of making gifts while you're alive. Make giving your possessions away a part of your annual gifting, especially if you're not using your things any more. Libby's grandmother gave a special piece of jewelry to each of her granddaughters on her wedding day. She had the joy of watching them wear a family heirloom as they walked down the aisle. Now each granddaughter has the fun of showing off her jewelry at black-tie events and other big occasions. As for the stuff that you no longer want and you don't think anyone else wants, get rid of it! Have a garage sale. Make a few dollars by selling items on eBay, because one person's junk is another person's treasure. And if it's just rubbish that's cluttering your closets and attic, throw it away! You'll have a fabulously clean house and you'll spare your nearest and dearest from throwing out cancelled checks from the 1950s and spending weeks discarding drawers full of debris. If the idea of cleaning out your possessions by yourself is too much, there are wonderful companies that will help you out, including determining what items have value (they'll help you sell them, too), what should be donated to charity, and what should be added to the dumpster.

Although it's not required, many individuals like to leave specific items of intangible property or certain

sums of money to particular friends or institutions. These are called either specific devises or specific bequests. Examples include leaving $25,000 to your university or $1,000 to each of your nieces and nephews. There's no limit to these gifts. They also don't have to be in cash. For instance, your bank account at XYZ Trust may be left to your sister or shares in a family business to your son who is following in your footsteps.

Some Wills include special directions for real property, whether it's the family homestead passing to a particular child or farmland passing to a conservancy charity, or a direction that the property be sold. If your real estate isn't specifically addressed, it's added to everything else and treated as part of your residuary estate.

The **residue** of your estate (also called your residuary estate) is everything you own at the time of your death, after all debts, taxes, expenses, and specific distributions have been paid, that is distributed according to your Will. In other words, your residuary estate is just that, everything you haven't already distributed to particular loved ones or organizations. The real planning begins with your residuary estate. It can pass to one person or charity, or to many people or many charities, or it can pass to a combination of the two. Most married women provide for their husband. If he's no longer alive, they provide that their estates pass to their children. Distributions to children can be **per capita** (in equal shares to your surviving children) or **per stirpes** (in equal shares to all of your children, with the share of a deceased child passing to his or her descendants). Maybe you have a partner you want to pass your estate

to. Or maybe you're a successful single who wants to care for your nieces and nephews, as well as your favorite charity.

Mini-Legal Dictionary

Here are a few legal terms that will help you understand estate planning basics:

Irrevocable—A legal document that can't be changed or revoked.

Revocable—A legal document that can be changed, amended, or cancelled.

Issue or descendants—All individuals born of a common ancestor. Your children, grandchildren, and great-grandchildren (and so on) are your issue or descendants.

Per capita—Division of an estate among a single branch of the family tree in which all members share and share alike. If you leave your estate to your children *per capita* and one of your children has already died, that child's share will be split among your living children.

Per stirpes—Division of an estate among all branches of a family tree. If you leave your estate to your children *per stirpes* and one of your children has already died, that child's share will pass to that child's children. This is also referred to as *by representation*.

Your residuary estate can be divided using percentages or equal shares. You should avoid using dollar amounts, because the end result could be drastically different from what you wanted if your estate increases or decreases dramatically.

Division Decisions

I always find examples to be extremely helpful. Here are a few ideas on different ways to divvy up your residuary estate:

1. One equal share for each child, with one share passing to each child then living and one share to each child who may be deceased but leaving behind surviving descendants.

2. 50 percent to your daughter, if she is living, and if not living, to her then living descendants, and 50 percent to your son, if he is then living, and if not then living, to his then living descendants.

3. 75 percent to your surviving nieces and nephews, to be divided equally, and 25 percent to your alma mater.

Once you've outlined who gets what and how much, you need to decide how the funds are received. You may want your adult beneficiaries to receive assets from your estate with no strings attached. This is an **outright distribution.** You can also create a Trust under your Will to hold assets for a certain number of years or until a beneficiary reaches a certain age.

We find that most married women and men want to leave everything to their spouse. While this is certainly simple and straightforward, it may not be the best plan for two reasons. Let's say Carol Brady died first and left everything to her handsome hubby, Mike Brady. Mike isn't the father of Marcia, Jan, and Cindy. So when Mike dies, if he leaves all of his assets to his children, only Greg, Peter, and Bobby will receive anything. The girls are out of luck. Or maybe Mike, despite his best intentions, loses all of Carol's money gambling, makes some bad investment decisions, or spends all his money bailing out his floundering architecture practice. In order to protect her girls, Carol would be well-advised to use a Trust. Mike would receive the income for life and principal could be distributed to him for his health, support, and maintenance. This way, Mike has the use of Carol's funds for life, and, on his death, Marcia, Jan, and Cindy are still taken care of because they receive the remainder of the Trust. It seems like just the kind of sensible plan Carol would consider.

Wills and Trusts—Aren't They the Same Thing?

A **Trust** is a separate legal entity that holds property for the benefit of someone or something. *Inter vivos* Trusts are established during the lifetime of the person creating the Trust. A Will directs how your possessions are passed on your passing. A Trust established under a Will is a Testamentary Trust.

A Trust for your husband also has some very important tax advantages. In Chapter 3 you read about the applicable exclusion from federal estate tax that each of us has. In 2008, that amount is $2,000,000. You can pass this amount to anyone without incurring any federal estate tax. There is also an unlimited marital deduction for assets that you pass to your husband, unless your husband isn't an American (more about that in a minute). If Carol Brady gives all of her money to Mike when she dies, there will be no federal estate tax due at her death. However, the amount Carol can pass to her daughters tax-free has been lost. Let me show you what I mean. Carol and Mike each have $2,000,000. If Carol leaves her entire $2,000,000 to Mike, there's no federal estate tax. But Mike now has $4,000,000. When Mike dies, his estate is worth $4,000,000, but he can only pass $2,000,000 free of federal estate tax. There could be as much as $900,000 in estate tax due from Mike's estate. Even someone who hates math knows that zero tax versus $900,000 of tax is a big difference.

Carol can avoid this taxing situation by using the same Trust for Mike. The entire $2,000,000 from Carol's estate would be held in Trust for Mike. Just like above, he'll receive the income and principal as needed. But at Mike's death, the $2,000,000 won't be included in his estate. In this situation, the Trust not only guarantees that Marcia, Jan, and Cindy will receive the remainder of the Trust, but that federal estate taxes on both Carol and Mike's estates will be reduced to zero. For Carol and for many of you, the use of a Trust is just a no-brainer.

Carol Brady's Last Will and Testament

I loved the Brady Bunch growing up. (Who didn't?) So, I thought the lovely Carol Brady's imaginary Will would be a great example. Because most Wills contain page after page of legalese, I'll just provide you with the highlights.

1. All expenses, debts, and taxes are paid by Carol's estate.

2. Carol provides that the infamous silver platter passes to Jan because Jan always felt slighted. Carol's jewelry passes in equal shares to Marcia, Jan, and Cindy. The rest of her personal property passes to Mike.

3. Carol provides that her share of that splendid split level home passes to Mike.

4. Carol leaves a specific bequest of $10,000 to each of Greg, Peter, and Bobby. She also leaves Alice $25,000 to go out and begin a new life with Sam the Butcher.

5. Carol provides that her entire estate be held in Trust for Mike if he survives her. On Mike's death the Trust, or her residuary estate if Mike doesn't survive her, passes in equal shares to Marcia, Jan, and Cindy, per stirpes. The share for any individual who hasn't turned 35 will be held in Trust for his or her benefit.

In legal circles, the Trust that Carol is setting up for Mike is called a **by-pass** or **credit shelter** Trust. There are also Trusts for spouses that qualify for the marital deduction. These Trusts are Qualified Terminable Interest Property Trusts, or QTIP Trusts. You can have one of each type of Trust for your husband if your assets exceed $2,000,000. Or, you can hold some of your assets in Trust and pass some assets outright to him. You can create a customized plan that works for your particular situation. Ask your attorney for advice.

If your groom has a passport from a country other than the USA, the unlimited marital deduction discussed above doesn't apply. If you leave property outright to him, you'll be using up your applicable exclusion from federal estate tax on your husband. An alternative is a **Qualified Domestic Trust** (QDOT). A QDOT provides income to your husband for life. Principal can be made available, but it could be subject to tax. The only catch is that the Trustee of the QDOT must be a U.S. citizen. In 2008, if the Trust is more than $2,000,000, one of the Trustees must be a U.S. bank or Trust company. Why these different rules? Uncle Sam is trying to keep your husband from leaving the U.S. with all of your money after you die.

By now you know that the tax laws not only keep changing, but are also likely to change some time soon. For that reason, many practitioners suggest that married couples with assets between $2,000,000 and $4,000,000 consider disclaimer Wills. A **disclaimer** is a legal term for saying, "Thanks, but no thanks," to a devise under a Will. In a disclaimer Will, you leave everything to your husband, outright and free from Trust. If your husband signs a disclaimer after you die, the assets you've provided for him instead pass into a Trust for his benefit. You're probably thinking, why would my husband ever agree to such a thing? He would because it may be the best decision for your family. At the time of your death, it allows your better half to consider your assets, his health, his needs, the needs of your family, and the current tax laws. It's flexible planning that's definitely worth considering. However, if you and your husband have children from different marriages, relationships, or otherwise contrary objectives, disclaimer planning probably isn't right for you.

You've probably noticed that I've only been talking about your husband with regard to the above Trusts. The U.S. only recognizes traditional, heterosexual marriages. Therefore, the benefits provided to a *husband* are only available to a *husband*. Some states provide tax benefits to lesbian and domestic partners; however, these benefits do not translate to the federal government.

After your husband, if you have children, they're probably next in line to receive benefits from your estate. I strongly believe that Trusts should be established for young children. Money, no matter how much or how little, in the hands of an 18-year-old usually translates to a fast car, lots of parties, and even more parties (can you say Paris Hilton?). A Trust for a child can provide for your wee one's health, support, maintenance, and education. You can provide that your offspring receive all the Trust income, or income only at the Trustee's discretion. The Trust can be for the lifetime of the child, or it can be distributed at certain ages that you think are right. I like using several different ages for distribution. This allows a child to adjust to receiving large sums of money and also allows your Trustee to see how he or she handles the funds. Partial distributions at ages 25 and 30, with the balance distributed at 35 is a favorite of most of my clients.

If you have a beneficiary who is disabled, talk to an attorney specializing in elder and disability planning. A Supplemental Benefits Trust may be perfect. Or, maybe you're simply trying to protect a loved one from his or her extravagant spending habits or the Trust funds from an unscrupulous spouse. Whatever your reasons, there are many options available, one of which is right for your loved one.

In creating your estate plan, I want to provide you with a word of caution. Avoid using your estate planning as a threat or weapon. I'm talking about the dramatic scenes in which a family matriarch on a daytime drama threatens to "cut you out of my Will." It's perfect for sappy soaps, but not for real life. These actions rarely result in the behaviors they're meant to encourage. Instead, such statements usually result in harboring destructive emotions and could be the basis for litigation after your death. The same holds true for trying to exert dead hand control in your Will or Trust. This is done by requiring certain actions by a beneficiary for him or her to receive distributions. The requirement might be marrying in a particular faith, attending a certain college, or visiting a family member's mausoleum annually (thank Leona Helmsley for that one!). Often, these requirements are deemed unenforceable, so why stir up the pot by including them?

And if there is someone you really want to exclude in your Will, exclude them. Make a statement that is clear: "I specifically exclude my granddaughter, Paris Hilton, from my Will and intend that she receive no benefit from my estate in any manner." This way, Ms. Hilton can't argue that she was mistakenly omitted from the Will. Don't say why you're excluding Paris; it just causes problems down the road. While there may be a temptation to leave out your husband, he may be eligible to receive a statutory elective share of your estate if you do exclude him (unless of course you have a prenuptial agreement). Get counsel from your attorney; there are other options.

One thing about my job, it's made me the queen of doomsday scenarios. I can give you examples of one bad thing after the next. For this reason, I encourage most of my clients to include a provision in their Wills or Trusts for a common disaster. This is the unlikely event that all of your beneficiaries die before you or you all die at the same time. It sounds cavalier to say this, but think of it as the family vacation plane crash. Because horrible things happen every day, be sure to include a list of beneficiaries if there is a common disaster. It could be nieces, nephews, charities, friends, or some combination. If you don't select these beneficiaries, they'll be determined by the laws of intestacy.

Do You Have to Have a Whole New Will to Make a Small Change?

No. If the change you want to make is minor, such as naming a different Executor or Guardian, you may use a Codicil. A **Codicil** is a properly executed legal document that changes part of an existing Will, without nullifying the entire Will.

As you're creating your estate plan, remember that your Will isn't irrevocable. You can change it any time you'd like. Don't hesitate to get moving because you're worried you'll be making a decision for life. The only time you can't change your Will is after your death or if you become incapacitated—just the times when you need to have your Will in place.

Trusts

Trust me. It's an expression we hear uttered all the time. What exactly does *trust* mean? It's often defined as "assured reliance on the character, ability, strength, or truth of someone or something." If you create a Trust, you're relying on a trusted individual or entity to safeguard your assets, either for yourself or for someone else.

What's a Trust?

A Trust is property that is managed by a Trustee for another person's benefit—the beneficiary. It's a method to safeguard assets for the beneficiary.

Generally, there are two types of Trusts: inter vivos (a Trust you create during life) and testamentary (a Trust created under your Will, like the Trusts we discussed earlier in this chapter). Trusts can be for yourself, your husband, your children, other loved ones, and for charities.

Hmmm...if you have a Will, why would you want to set up a Trust? You've probably heard of *probate*. A court proceeding that proves a Last Will and Testament to be valid or invalid is **probate**. You've probably also heard people say that you need to do anything you can to avoid probate. That's because in some states probate is expensive, with probate costs tied to the value of the estate. In these states, such as Florida, California, New York, and Massachusetts, the probate process is terribly time-consuming and difficult, with an inordinate amount of court involvement. In other states, probate is very simple, inexpensive, and easy.

You Have a Trust, Do You Still Need a Will?

Absolutely! A Will is always a good idea, even if you've transferred all of your assets into a Trust. We've discovered that there's always some small asset that wasn't transferred to the Trust. Without a Will, transferring it on your death could be difficult. So it's best to cover all your bases and have both documents. Your Will can simply provide that any assets not already in your Trust be added to your Trust. Besides, if you have tiny children, you still need a Will to name their Guardians.

If you live in one of the probate un-friendly states, you'll likely be counseled to place your assets into a **Revocable Living Trust** (also called a **Grantor Trust** or **Living Trust**). A Revocable Living Trust states that while you're alive, you can change, amend, or revoke the Trust. You're also entitled to all the Trust income and the entire Trust principal as you need it or request it. The assets in the Trust are transferred from your name into the name of the Trust. There is no tax ramification to this Trust as long as you're the sole beneficiary. In fact, the Trust uses your social security number as its taxpayer identification number. You, or any one you would like, may serve as the Trustee. As far as you're concerned, you've not given up any assets or control.

On your death, your Revocable Living Trust becomes irrevocable. The person or bank you designated to be the Trustee then distributes the Trust as you've provided. The provisions after your death are just like those found in a Will. They may include specific bequests or devises, and disposition of your real estate. The Trust may continue for your husband or children, or be distributed outright. There should be a common disaster clause as well. The benefit is that, because your assets are already in your Trust, there is no need for probate. The Trust is already considered valid because you declared it as such while you were alive.

The Law Against Perpetuity

In many states, there are old laws on the books that prevent Trusts from going on forever. The Law Against Perpetuity usually provides that a Trust must end 21 years after the death of the last individual alive at the death of the individual establishing the Trust. In layman's terms, unless you provide otherwise, the Trust you set up can't go on forever.

Trusts aren't limited to Revocable Living Trusts and Trusts you create under your Will. Trusts can be established during your lifetime to provide for your grandchildren's education or to benefit your favorite charity. There are Trusts to own real estate and Trusts to provide for disabled beneficiaries. We'll talk more about these and Charitable Trusts, Asset Protection Trusts, Insurance Trusts, Personal Residence Trusts, and other estate planning options in Chapter 7, "What If You Want to Get Fancy with Your Planning?"

Beneficiary Designations

A large percentage of asset transfers are made by beneficiary designation. As you recall, life insurance, 401(k)s, and IRAs, for example, often pass as you designate, no matter what your Will or Trust says. That's why it's so important to discuss your beneficiary designations with your lawyer to be sure they complement your plan and don't jeopardize everything you've worked so hard to put down on paper.

You can establish a terrific Trust for your kids; but if your life insurance is payable to them outright, well, that kind of defeats the purpose of keeping lots of money out of their hands at an early age. The same is true for retirement benefits. If it's payable to them directly, that could be a great deal of cash in the hands of an impressionable young adult. There are also many income tax implications to retirement benefits, so it's especially important to sit down with an expert to discuss the details.

Be sure to ask your lawyer questions about your particular beneficiary designation assets and what you can do with them, such as having them pass to a see-through Trust or other type of Trust.

Meeting Your Attorney

You've got the attorney appointment scheduled. You should bring your significant other, right? Usually, the answer is, "Yes." But for some, maybe it's not such a great idea. Maybe you're cohabiting or your current husband isn't the father of your children. If that's the case, you should probably attend the meeting alone. Why? Your husband and your children could be considered to have competing interests. Or, maybe you've got kids who fight like cats and dogs or a child that you'll be leaving out of your Will or Trust for a whole host of reasons. Both of these scenarios are good reasons to leave your offspring out of the meeting. It's also wise to use your own lawyer. Don't use the same attorney as your favorite son—it could be argued that there's a conflict of interest, thereby causing problems down the road. If you can act today to avoid a problem later, do it. That includes using independent counsel. It's wise, prudent, and good planning—especially because it's *your* planning.

You've probably noticed that I keep referring to your lawyer, counselor, and attorney. That's because I've seen firsthand the problems that are created when people prepare "do it yourself" Wills and Trusts. Yes, you can find Will and Trust forms online and in those big office stores. However, as the old saying goes, you get what you pay for. I could fill dozens of pages outlining the problems caused when homemade Wills are left behind. The money saved by not visiting a lawyer in the first place is now lost, often many times over, with the requirement of lawyers, court actions, and miscommunicated and misunderstood wishes. The procedure for signing a Will, to be sure it's valid, varies from state to state. Some states require two witnesses, others require three. The language for having a self-proving Will (which keeps your loved ones from having to locate the witnesses to your Will) is also different in every state. When you sign a Will, be sure it will be accepted in the state in which you live. If you move, be sure to have your Will reviewed by an attorney in your new home state. Of course, having your Will prepared by a lawyer is best. However, at the very least, have an attorney review any Will you've prepared and ask him or her to assist with the Will's execution. Bottom line: Paying a lawyer today will likely save legal and court fees when you die.

If legal fees are a big concern, reduce the bill by being prepared for your meeting. Do your research. Bring typed or neatly printed information (or send it by e-mail or on a disk or memory card), provide details, and know what you want. There is nothing that creates a big legal bill more than a couple, for example, fighting in front of the lawyer. I've sat patiently with clients who've screamed at one another for almost an hour over who should be the Guardian for their minor children. Despite my reminding them that the clock was ticking, they kept at it. In the end, they had a high bill and high blood pressure; and I had an hour of wasted time. So unless you're looking to spend as much as possible for legal advice (personally, I'd rather spend that money at the mall), get your thoughts together before you arrive for your meeting.

Many lawyers will ask you to complete an estate planning questionnaire or information form before your appointment. If not, I suggest that you bring the following details along with you:

1. Your full legal name and any aliases.
2. Your legal address.
3. Your social security number.
4. Your citizenship.
5. Your husband or domestic partner's full legal name (and aliases), address, citizenship, and social security number.
6. If you're widowed, your late husband's name and date of death.

7. If you're divorced, your former husband's name and divorce date. Also bring along a copy of any Property Settlement or similar agreement. This will help your lawyer determine if any additional planning is required by the document.

8. Name of your accountant, if any. Let your lawyer know if you want your accountant to be included in the planning process.

9. Name of your financial advisor, if any. Let your attorney know if you want your financial advisor to be involved in the planning process.

10. Any pre-nuptial or ante-nuptial agreements.

11. Name, address, and age of your children, grandchildren, and all other beneficiaries. Include your relationship to each individual.

12. Names of your parents and any potential inheritance.

13. The You're Worth It Statement prepared in Chapter 2. Include both your assets and your liabilities.

14. Bring copies of beneficiary designations for your life insurance, IRAs, 401(k)s, and any other asset that has such a designation.

15. If you're a beneficiary of any Trust, bring along a copy of the Trust agreement if you have it. This includes any Trusts created by a late husband, parent, or grandparent.

16. Copies of any gift tax returns (IRS Form 709) you may have filed. If you haven't filed any gift tax returns, make a list of any big gifts or loans

you may have made. Use $10,000 as the trigger point. Make a list of all transfers you've made of more than $10,000 or totaling more than $10,000 in any calendar year. If you signed or joined in any gift tax returns of a husband or former husband, inform your counselor.

17. A list of any specific or charitable bequests you'd like to make; for example, $1,000 to each grandchild or $10,000 to your alma mater. Provide exact legal names and addresses.

18. A brief summary of your estate planning goals. Your summary might say you'd like to provide for your significant other for life and then provide for your children. Or, maybe you want to skip one child and provide for your grandkids instead. Perhaps you're only interested in benefiting charitable organizations. Write down what you're thinking to help point your counselor (and you) in the right direction.

19. A list of your concerns and anything else that's important to you. If it troubles you, write it down. Maybe you have a son-in-law that makes you nervous with his crazy business schemes. Maybe your granddaughter is behaving like Paris Hilton. Others may be worried about a daughter's drinking or drug problem. Tell your lawyer everything! Don't wait until the documents are drafted to mention that your grandson has special needs. Redrafting documents is costly, both in legal fees and your time.

20. Names and addresses of the individuals to serve as your Executor or Personal Representative, Trustee, and Guardian, as well as at least two successors for each position.

21. Information for the preparation of a Power of Attorney, Health Care Proxy, and Living Will (see Chapter 8, "What If You Get Sick and Can't Make Decisions?").

Tell your attorney everything. As I like to say, problems cannot be resolved unless problems are identified. You may be embarrassed about this or that (aren't we all a little ashamed of something?). But trust me, your lawyer doesn't care. Not sharing your concerns can result in an estate plan that is ineffective. I'd rather learn today that you and your brother just can't get along so we can plan accordingly. Lay all your cards on the table. You may be surprised at the wonderful ideas your lawyer gives you.

Estate Planning To Do List

If you're like me, you love To Do lists. The following is your To Do list when you sit down with your estate planning counselor. Make sure you cross everything off your list before you leave his or her office!

1. Provide the name and address of the individual or institution, as well as at least two successors, that you want to serve as your Executor.

2. Provide the name and address of the individual or institution, and at least two successors, to serve as your Trustee.

---

3. Provide the name and address of the Guardian, and two successor Guardians, of your minor or disabled children.

4. Outline the small or specific bequests or devises you'd like to make. Be sure to give your attorney the full legal name and address of each beneficiary.

5. Discuss the beneficiaries of your estate and how you would like them to receive their inheritance. Provide their full legal names and addresses, as well as your relationship to the beneficiaries. Be sure to tell your attorney if any beneficiary is a minor, disabled, or not a U.S. citizen.

6. Provisions for your common disaster clause. Include full legal names and addresses.

7. Name and address of your Agent under a Power of Attorney, as well as two successor Agents (see Chapter 8 for more details).

8. Name and address of your Health Care Representative under a Health Care Proxy, as well as two successor Health Care Representatives (see Chapter 8 for more details).

9. Your wants and wishes at the end of life and any religious language to be contained in your Living Will (see Chapter 8 for more details).

Make your attorney's job easier by being organized and prepared. He or she will appreciate your efforts and so will you. (Can you say smaller bill?)

I know it's a lot to think about, but there's even more. Keep reading to learn more about what you can do to reduce your estate taxes and provide for your family.

What Should You Do Next?

1. Outline your estate planning goals.
2. Gather and organize all the information your counselor will need.
3. Tell your lawyer *everything*!

Chapter 7

What If You Want to Get Fancy with Your Planning?

The simplest plan can save your loved ones heart-aches and headaches. For many, basic planning can often save lots of tax dollars. So, what if you're fortunate enough to have an estate that has lots of zeros at the end? Lucky for you, there are many ter-rific and effective estate planning vehicles to discuss with your attorney. One or more may be right for you and your loved ones. The benefits are twofold: tax dol-lars saved and goals achieved. Now that's what I call a win-win situation!

Sharing the Wealth

In Chapter 6 ("What's a Will? What's a Trust? How Do You Use Them to Put Your Plan in Place?"), we talked about the significant tax savings you get when you leave some or all of your assets in Trust for your husband. It's the simplest way to use your applicable exclusion from federal estate tax ($2,000,000 in 2008 and $3,500,000 in 2009) and still take care of your groom. You can also provide that these funds pass directly to your children, with your other assets passing to your husband. The key, though, is that you must have enough assets in your name alone to do this. As you learned in Chapter 2 ("What Exactly Does Your Estate Include?"), joint assets and assets with a beneficiary designation pass to the surviving tenant or the designated beneficiary, no matter what your estate planning documents say.

If you don't already have property in your individual name, but you own it jointly with your husband, break the tenancy on your joint assets. What does this mean? It means changing your joint accounts and real estate to tenants-in-common. This means that your share of each asset will pass as you've planned, not directly to your partner. It also gives you enough assets to fully use up your exclusion amount. Because that amount is so valuable, it's critical to do this.

In some families, just because of who worked out of the home and who worked at home, one partner has much more money than the other. Traditionally, this was the man of the house (although, with younger families, it could be either partner). In this case, and I know it won't be easy, your other half needs to transfer some money into your name so you both have enough funds for tax planning purposes. Just like an unlimited deduction for estate tax purposes, there is an unlimited deduction for gifts between spouses. Going back to the Brady Bunch example, if Mike has all the money in his name and Carol dies first with no money in her name, Carol's $2,000,000 exclusion is lost forever. The result is $900,000 in tax instead of zero. Even the tightest tight wad can recognize the tax benefits of forking over some of his dough. Keep after him until he gets it done!

It Is Better to Give Than to Receive

As I've already admitted, I love holidays and birthdays. Nothing makes me happier than buying and wrapping gifts for my nearest and dearest. But there's another reason I love gifts. As you learned in Chapter 3 ("Is It Really *That* Important to Think About Taxes?"), gifts are, without a doubt, wonderful and effective estate planning tools. Most of the fancy planning we'll be discussing in this chapter focuses on making gifts today in some form or another.

Taxing Gifts

No, I don't mean those gifts that stress you out as you wait in line at 4 a.m. for the must-have toy for your favorite wee one. I mean those gifts that could result in gift tax. That's right: Gifts in excess of the annual exclusion from gift tax ($12,000 in 2008) are considered taxable gifts requiring the filing of a gift tax return.

As with any lifetime estate planning, you have to be comfortable making gifts. You'll be giving up control over the gifts you make. You also won't be able to use the money you give away. Making gifts, despite all the benefits, shouldn't be taken lightly. You have to want to do it. And, you must be able to afford gift-giving. It's also important to talk to your husband, if you're married, about the gifts you make. He may be willing to join in your gifts, allowing you to give away more.

Incentive and Other Trusts

Taking care of your kids, grandkids, or other small ones in your life is important. How you do it is just as important. I've made it clear throughout this book that I don't believe in young children receiving large sums of money. When you create a Trust (whether during your life or at death) for the tiny tots in your life, think carefully about the ages at which they should receive the Trust funds outright and free from Trust. Some folks think 30 is the perfect age. Others like 50. It's up to you and what you think is best for your beneficiaries. You can also provide that funds be held in Trust for the lifetime of your child. This is especially important if your son or daughter has trouble managing money, is easily influenced by a spouse or partner, or has other afflictions.

For many moms, they're very worried about the "brat factor." How do they keep their kids from acting like Paris Hilton with a sense of entitlement and a Trust Fund mentality? One effective Trust is the **Incentive Trust**. In this Trust, you provide that the beneficiary only receive distributions equal to what he or she earns in the real world. If your granddaughter earns $100,000 a year, she receives $100,000 from her Trust. If your grandson is a slacker and earns nothing, he receives nothing. Provision can be included for beneficiaries that have socially responsible jobs (for example, a teacher in an inner-city school) or are sick, disabled, or otherwise unable to earn a living as determined by the Trustee. Again, you can create a Trust that reflects your values and hopes for your beneficiaries and doesn't just hand them a silver spoon.

Generation Skipping Trusts

Spoiling your grandkids doesn't have to be limited to trains, dolls, swing sets, and stuffed animals. You can set up Trusts today for their education, or simply as an account to invest the annual exclusion gifts you give them every year (hint hint!). **Generation Skipping Trusts** can also be created to utilize your exclusion from the generation skipping transfer (GST) tax. A GST Trust usually provides for your children during their lifetimes, and then passes to your grandchildren without being taxed in your child's estate. It's a way to avoid a layer of double-taxation (taxed in your estate, then in your child's estate before making its way to the next generation) and is the reason the IRS caps what you can skip to the next generation. A GST Trust can be very beneficial in transferring large sums of wealth to another generation. It is, however, also complicated. Talk to your counselor to learn more.

Life Insurance and Life Insurance Trusts

Many of you have life insurance, whether it's the group term policy through your employer or a term policy you bought to help pay off the mortgage in the event of an early death. Today, life insurance can be a sound financial investment as well. Many of you know that the proceeds of a life insurance policy (the face value of the policy that your loved ones receive when you die) usually aren't income to the beneficiary, and therefore, aren't subject to income tax. What you may not know is that the same life insurance proceeds are considered an asset of your estate for estate tax purposes if you own and control the life insurance policy. You own and control the policy if you can modify the terms of the policy, assign the policy, and change the policy beneficiaries. In other words, if you die in 2008, the proceeds of the policy you own and control could be taxed up to 45 percent depending on your other assets.

The alternative to owning and controlling a life insurance policy is to have the policy owned and controlled by an **Irrevocable Life Insurance Trust**. The key here is *irrevocable*. Once the policy is transferred to a Life Insurance Trust or you consent to the Trust purchasing insurance on your life, the policy is out of your reach and control and therefore is not included in your estate for estate tax purposes. You must be comfortable with this irrevocability. Keep in mind that if you die within three years of transferring an existing policy to a Trust, the policy will still be included in your estate. So if you make this kind of transfer, you can't go anywhere for three years!

Life Insurance Quick Tax Calculation

It's 2008. You've worked hard and saved hard. Your total assets are $3,000,000. You also own a life insurance policy naming your kids as beneficiaries. The face value of the policy is $2,000,000. Doing a quick calculation, your total estate is now $5,000,000. The federal estate tax due on this amount is $1,350,000 if you die in 2008. If the life insurance was owned by an Irrevocable Life Insurance Trust, the tax due would be $450,000. Kind of makes the decision easy, don't you agree?

A Life Insurance Trust owns the life insurance policy. You make a gift to the Trust whenever life insurance premiums are due. When you die, the life insurance is paid to the Trust and distributed as you've provided in the Trust. Usually, the funds provide income and principal for your husband and descendants. When your husband dies, the Trust assets can be distributed to your kids or held in further Trust if your kids are still young. Your family benefits from the insurance policy just as they would if it weren't in a Trust. Really, they benefit more because there's no tax. You can do this with a single life insurance policy or with a joint and survivor policy (this is a life insurance policy that insures both your life and your husband's and pays out on the second death).

While life insurance isn't for everyone, it can provide great benefits if you have what we call an *illiquid estate*. This is an estate that is mostly made up of real estate or a small business—items your loved ones wouldn't want to sell, but would be forced to sell just to pay taxes because your estate has limited cash. Talk to a financial planner for information about the ways that life insurance can benefit your estate.

Residence Trusts

One of my favorite planning tools is the QPRT, or **Qualified Personal Residence Trust**. A QPRT is a Trust that lasts for a term of years. For the purposes of our discussion, let's say ten years. When you create a QPRT, you transfer your personal residence (whether it's your main home or a vacation home) to the Trust. During the ten-year term of the Trust, you use the residence as you always have. You pay the taxes and make the repairs. At the end of the ten-year term, the residence is transferred to your beneficiaries. You'll have no interest in the house at all, but you can lease it from the new owners (usually your children) for fair market rent.

When you create the Trust, you've made a gift to the Trust beneficiaries. The value of the gift, though, isn't the value of your residence. It's the value today of your residence when your loved ones receive it in ten years. The actual gift is determined using actuarial tables and the IRS Section 7520 rate, which is set monthly by the IRS. In financial circles, this is called the present value of a future gift. Your gift is more than the discounted current value of your home; you're also giving away today all the future appreciation on your residence. The benefits can be astronomical.

I'll give you an example. Caroline owned a beach house on Nantucket that was worth about a million dollars when she set up a QPRT in 1997. The discounted value of the gift for gift tax purposes was about $200,000 (the 1997 value of the $1,000,000 beach house the kids would receive in 2007). When the QPRT term ended ten years later in 2007, the beach house was worth $4,000,000 with Caroline's kids now owning the home. Because Caroline had other assets, the full $4,000,000 would have been taxed at 45 percent at her death. She saved more than $1,800,000 in estate taxes by making a gift valued at $200,000. Now that's what I consider great planning.

Grantor Retained Annuity Trusts

Like a QPRT, a **Grantor Retained Annuity Trust**, or GRAT, is a Trust for a term of years, whether it's one, five, or ten years. With a GRAT, you contribute assets to the Trust and then invest them. Each year, you, as the creator of the Trust, take a percentage distribution from the Trust. At the end of the term you've selected, whatever is left passes to the Trust's remainder beneficiaries. The goal here is to use highly appreciable assets so that the appreciation on the invested assets passes to your nearest and dearest without it being a big gift.

Here's a quick example. You invest $1,000,000 in a two-year GRAT. Each year you pay yourself 50 percent of the Trust. In the first year, the $1,000,000 grows by 20 percent to $1,200,000. You take out your required

50 percent (valued on the first day of the Trust), or $500,000, leaving $700,000 in the Trust. The remaining Trust assets continue to grow, this time by 30 percent. At the end of the second year, the Trust is now worth $910,000. You take out your required 50 percent of the original contribution, or $500,000. Your beneficiaries receive the difference of $410,000. If you're a talented investor, a GRAT is worth considering.

Charitable Trusts and Private Foundations

Charitable planning, as we've talked about, provides some wonderful benefits to the charities you love, as well as to your bottom line. In addition to outright gifts, gifts to your favorite charities may be made using Trusts.

When you establish a **Charitable Remainder Trust**, you receive the income from the invested assets for your lifetime or for a specific number of years. You'll receive an income tax deduction on creation of the Trust. On your death, or on the expiration of the specified term, the Trust funds pass to the charities you've selected. Even better, any low basis assets that you own may be sold in the Trust without incurring any capital gains tax. Low basis, or highly appreciated, securities are those securities that would result in a big capital gain if you sold them. Your basis is the price you paid for a stock or the value when you inherited or otherwise received the stock. For example, if Carol Brady purchased one share of Alice Co. for $1.00, and that share is now worth $200.00, Alice Co. would be a low basis security.

The opposite of a Charitable Remainder Trust is a **Charitable Lead Trust**. With this Trust, the charity receives the income from the Trust for a certain number of years. When the term of years ends, the Trust proceeds will be paid to the remainder beneficiaries. If the remainder beneficiary isn't you or your spouse, this will likely be a taxable gift when you create the Trust. Again, you'll receive an income tax deduction when the Trust is created and no capital gains will be recognized when low basis securities are sold and reinvested.

You can also set up a Charitable Trust for another person while you're alive or under your Will or Trust. If you set up this kind of Trust for someone else, there will be some gift or estate tax due, but it will be significantly less than an outright gift to your loved one.

Private foundations, although administratively burdensome, are terrific for teaching your family the value of philanthropy. Private foundations may be established as either a Trust or a corporation and are designed to invest the property you contribute. You do receive an income tax deduction for your contributions. Each year, the private foundation must give away at least five percent of its value to qualified charities. The decision as to what charities receive the foundation's good will is made by the private foundation's board. You can serve on the board, as well as your children and even your grandchildren if they're old enough. You can teach them what's important to you with real dollars and responsibilities. After you die, the foundation continues with your family in charge.

If you like the idea of a private foundation, but just don't want the headaches, try a donor-advised fund. They're available through community foundations and certain financial institutions.

Individual Retirement Accounts

IRAs are just one of the assets you may own with a beneficiary designation. For many of us, we started IRAs at a young age with the rollover of the 401(k) from our first job or with our first savings. The problem with IRAs is that they're expensive assets to die with. Why? Not only are they taxed for estate and inheritance tax purposes, but they're also subject to income tax when IRA assets are withdrawn. This means that, depending on the tax rates, your heirs could receive as little as 30 cents of every dollar of your retirement savings.

If you're charitable, naming a charity as the beneficiary of your IRA is a great idea. You benefit a favorite organization and your estate receives an estate tax deduction for the value of the IRA. Let's go back to the Brady family for our example. Greg is extremely successful selling Brady Bunch memorabilia and stashes away $1,000,000 in his IRA. He also has other assets, so the entire value of the IRA is taxable at his death. If Greg leaves the IRA to his brothers, Peter and Bobby, it is subject to a 45 percent federal estate tax rate. Because the IRA needs to be liquidated to pay the tax, income tax of, let's say 30 percent, must be paid. That's a total of 75 percent tax, with the remaining Brady brothers receiving only about $250,000. Instead, if Greg left the whole IRA to his favorite charity, he will have made a $1,000,000 donation with the $250,000 that would have gone to his brothers after taxes. Sure, Peter and Bobby will lose out on that quarter of a million dollars, but they've got their own reality shows and hopefully are diligent savers like their older brother.

For many of us, we've saved up so we can share our savings with our families. Your IRA can be distributed directly to your kids. In that situation, they can draw down the IRA using the life expectancy of your oldest child. If they don't withdraw all the money in one lump sum, they can stretch the benefits of the IRA out for years to come. Of course, any death taxes due should be paid from other assets. You can, alternatively, provide that the IRA be distributed to your husband, to be used during his lifetime. The problem with either of these options is that the IRA could be liquidated and all the tax due now with poor planning or greedy beneficiaries.

You might be tempted to name your estate or Trust as your beneficiary. But that's not such a great idea either. Why? If an estate or Trust is a beneficiary, the IRA must be distributed over a five-year period, meaning that the income tax you're trying to stretch out must be paid at some point over the next half decade. What you can do is use what's called a **see-through Trust**, which provides that the annual IRA distributions be paid to the Trust. These distributions must then be distributed to the beneficiary to maintain the *stretch* or tax deferral benefits of the IRA. It's a good solution if your heirs don't understand the benefits of keeping the IRA in effect for their lifetimes.

Asset Protection Trusts

The big buzz phrase in estate planning today is *asset protection*. How can you protect your assets from your creditors and your kid's creditors? Although there are offshore Trusts, several states provide better asset protection than others depending on the terms of the Trust. A great deal of discretion must be given to the Trustee, with the creator of the Trust required to give up all control, and the Trust must be irrevocable. The goal of such Trusts is to make it tough for creditors to get to your assets. **Asset Protection Trusts** only work before there is a problem. Setting up such a Trust after your husband files for divorce or after a serious accident will likely be ineffective and considered a sham, or fraudulent, transaction. If you're concerned about liability and are willing to giving up control, talk more with your lawyer about what you can do.

Family Limited Partnerships and Limited Liability Companies

Family Limited Partnerships (FLPs) and **Limited Liability Companies** (LLCs) are entities you create that operate just like a business. You would own all of the FLP or LLC, unless you decided to give some of it away. The benefit to making gifts of your FLP or LLC, or of any business you own, is that each unit you give away isn't worth as much as it might seem. Rather, the gift is discounted because it is a minority interest and unmarketable. In other words, you can't sell it to just anyone because of restrictions on transferring the shares or units. Discounts are determined by obtaining a formal valuation.

The benefits can be substantial. Here's an example. A share of your LLC is made up of assets worth $10,000. Because each share is a minority interest and has no market, it's discounted by 25 percent. This means that the gift you're making is valued at $7,500 for gift tax purposes. The same discounts may be applied to the shares you own at your death. In other words, you can give more for less. There are pros and cons to FLPs and LLCs, including increased review by the IRS. You need sound advice from an expert to learn more.

Fancy planning is more than just fancy. It's complicated and complex. This chapter provides just a taste of what you can do. You need the guidance of qualified professionals. Talk to your attorney to learn his or her ideas for your situation. Not only will your planning reduce taxes, but it will also make sure what you want to have happen does, in fact, happen.

What Should You Do Next?

1. Review your assets to determine if any fancy planning is right for you.

2. Assess your control tolerance. How much control and how much money are you willing to give up today to save tax dollars in the future?

3. Consider your long-term goals. How much do you want your children to receive? What about your grandchildren? Does philanthropy play a part in your planning?

Chapter 8

What If You Get Sick and Can't Make Decisions?

U nfortunately, many of us will face illness during our lives. Maybe it will be our own illness, or maybe it will be a friend's or loved one's. Hopefully it will be a short-term sickness with no lasting side effects. It could, however, also be an accident with life-threatening injuries. No matter what happens, there may come a time when we need help managing our affairs. I'm not talking about the neighbor who picks up the mail or a colleague who drops off a lasagna. Instead, I'm talking about assistance managing your finances and making medical decisions if you are unable to make decisions for yourself. Luellen, age 38, agrees that estate planning should always "include planning for those circumstances when you can no longer speak for yourself because if there is no Living Will or Health Care Proxy, the law might make presumptions about health care decisions," which is probably the last thing you want.

Who's the Helper and Who's the Helpee?

Agent or Attorney-in-Fact—The individual or individuals named to make your financial and business decisions under a Power of Attorney.

Health Care Representative—The individual or individuals named to make your health care and medical decisions under a Health Care Proxy.

Principal—The individual signing the Power of Attorney or Health Care Proxy and asking an Agent or Health Care Representative to make decisions on her behalf—in other words, you!

Deciding who you want to act on your behalf can be a very difficult decision. If you're lucky, the choice is obvious. Maybe you're married or in a committed relationship and your significant other understands what is important to you. You may want him or her to have the ability to make the choices you would have if you were able. For some, though, the decision isn't easy. I have single friends who don't have close relationships with family members, but don't want to burden friends. And, for some, they love their kids, but don't think they are capable of making tough decisions.

If you find yourself struggling with who to select, I recommend studying your nearest and dearest. Who do you trust to make the same decisions you would? I'll give you the same rule of thumb I gave you in Chapter 4 ("Who Makes Sure Everything You Want to Have Happen Happens When You're Gone?") for selecting an Executor or Trustee: Pick the individual or individuals who are smart enough to ask for help. We all have gut instincts—follow them! If the thought of naming a certain person makes you uncomfortable, there's a reason. Pick someone else. Don't worry about what you think you should do. Select the person you know, deep down inside, is the right person for the job. If you're concerned that you'll hurt someone's feelings or cause a rift in the family, leave a short note explaining your decision. While it may be tempting to ignore the decision, that's even worse. Your loved ones could be prohibited from making any decisions or, alternatively, may be forced to go to court for a judge to decide who should make the decisions on behalf of Grandma. Just the thought of a public hearing should be enough to encourage you to pick someone!

Power of Attorney

Powers of Attorney are fairly commonplace. Chances are you've signed one for a limited purpose, maybe for a real estate sale. Maybe you read about it with regard to New York City socialite Brooke Astor and her son's alleged abuse of her Power of Attorney. A **Power of Attorney** is an extremely useful document. It can be beneficial when you're feeling fine (for example, your Agent can make stock trades for you or pay your bills when you're on an around the world first class cruise!) or when you're sick or injured and unable to write checks, file your taxes, or otherwise conduct your financial affairs.

There are three types of Powers of Attorney: Spring-ing, Limited, and General. A Springing Power of Attor-ney is only effective when the Principal is incapacitated. Usually this requires the findings of two licensed physi-cians. While the Springing Power of Attorney may seem perfect, it is very inconvenient for your named Agent to obtain notes from doctors and to then trot them around to the many financial institutions at which you have accounts. Alternatively, the General and Limited Powers of Attorney are active upon signing, which means that you do not have to be incapacitated or unable to act at such time as your Agent under the Power of Attorney seeks to act. Yikes, maybe you're thinking, "I'm not so sure I want my Agent to be able to access my account today, when I'm feeling great and am more than able to manage my affairs." While that may be true, if you can't trust your Agent today, he or she shouldn't serve as your Agent at any time.

The distinction between the General and Limited Power of Attorney is how much power you're giving your Agent. A General Power of Attorney lets your Agent do just about everything you could do if you were able to act. Just as you can sell real estate and personal property, create Trusts, resign appointments, enter your safe deposit box, make gifts, file taxes, make deposits, and sell stocks, under a General Power of Attorney, your Agent can also do all of these things. The only thing your Agent can't do is make health care decisions for you or request information about your health or medical care.

Unlike a General Power of Attorney, a Limited Power of Attorney is just that, limited. This document specifies particular, limited acts to be performed by your Agent. Maybe you want your Agent to make bank deposits and pay bills, but don't want your Agent to have the power to sell any of your assets. Because none of us can predict what happens tomorrow, a General Power of Attorney is always best because we just don't know when we'll need help or what kind of help we'll need. If you don't have a trusted individual to act on your behalf, or if you have other concerns, talk to your attorney. He or she may have other ideas for your particular apprehensions and circumstances. For example, if you're worried about providing a fully active General Power of Attorney to your Agent today, ask your attorney to hold all of the original documents in his or her file pursuant to a Holding Letter. In this letter, you ask your law firm to keep your original Power of Attorney until your Agent provides evidence of your incapacity and your lawyer is satisfied that you are in fact incapacitated.

It's also very important that both the General and Limited Power of Attorney be *durable*. The Power of Attorney should specifically state that it remains valid and in full effect even when you become incapacitated or unable to act. Without such language specifying durability, it might be argued that the Power of Attorney is no longer effective when you're incapacitated, which is exactly what you're trying to avoid. Double check with your counselor to confirm that your Power of Attorney is durable.

The ABCs of General Durable Powers of Attorney

A General Durable Power of Attorney lets your Agent act from A to Z on your behalf. The document should outline exactly what you're authorizing your Agent to do, in addition to the powers authorized by the laws of the state in which you live and a general power to do everything you could do if you were able. The powers of your Agent could include the following:

1. Conducting all banking transactions, including depositing and withdrawing funds and making electronic or wire transfers.

2. Opening, closing, and maintaining bank, brokerage, or other accounts.

3. Buying and selling securities of any kind.

4. Opening, closing, and entering safe deposit boxes.

5. Spending funds on behalf of dependents.

6. Loaning or borrowing funds and collecting debts.

7. Collecting funds, including interest and dividends.

8. Voting Proxies.

9. Purchasing and disposing of real and personal property.

10. Making gifts.

11. Creating, revoking, or amending Trust agreements.

12. Preparing and filing tax returns.

> **13.** Changing beneficiary forms.
>
> **14.** Resigning or renouncing appointments, dis-claiming interests in property, hiring persons, or engaging services of any kind.

Maybe you're thinking, "I'm not comfortable, so I'll just pass on the Power of Attorney." As tempting as that may be, it's a big mistake. Why? As noted previously, at some time in the future you may need help, whether the help is temporary or permanent. You could need help paying your taxes, selling property, trading stocks, and making other financial decisions. Without appointing someone to make these decisions now—while you're still able—your family and friends could be forced to request court involvement to adjudicate the appropriate person or persons to act for you.

I'll give you my favorite example. Tomorrow you're hit by a bus, which causes you to fall into a coma. In other words, you're incapacitated. If you don't have a valid Power of Attorney, a court could appoint a Guardian to act on your behalf. The court-appointed Guardian would make both financial and health care decisions for you. Depending on the extent of your inca-pacity, a court could appoint a Conservator to handle your finances only. Every state has a different definition of the role of a Conservator or Guardian. No matter what type of court proceeding there is, a Guardian ad litem would probably be appointed to act on your behalf. Just to make things confusing, this guardian is different from the permanent Guardian a court would appoint or the Guardian you name for your minor or disabled children. The role of a **Guardian ad litem** is to protect your interests during a Court action and to assist in determining if you really are incapacitated, if a Guardian or Conservator should be appointed for you, and to make a recommendation as to who should serve for you. Because the appointment of a Guardian or Conservator is a public proceeding, information about you (such as your finances and medical condition) becomes a matter of public record. Add to that the cost of these proceedings in both time and money. And, not to keep mentioning control, but if there is a time in the future when you need someone to act on your behalf, shouldn't you pick that person? As you can tell, having a Power of Attorney in place is critical.

Advance Directives—Living Wills and Health Care Proxies

No doubt you've heard the following statement, or said it yourself: "Don't keep me hooked up to machines, just pull the plug." For most of my friends and clients, this is their choice. They can say it in a number of different ways, but the sentiment is the same: Don't keep me around if I'm really, really sick and won't live much longer any way.

But, as the adage goes, "Saying it and doing it are two different things." You need binding legal documents that state exactly what medical care you want and don't want, as well as a directive as to who should act on your behalf. With these in place, there should be no questions regarding your end of life care.

Because they can be completed in a number of different ways, health care documents can be confusing. The **Health Care Proxy**, also called a Durable Power of Attorney for Health Care, Medical Power of Attorney, and Advance Directive for Health Care—Proxy Directive, appoints a Health Care Representative to act on your behalf. The **Living Will**, also called an **Advance Directive for Health Care—Instruction Directive**, outlines your wishes with regard to medical care at the end of life. These can be two separate documents or combined into a single document. You can have a Living Will without a Health Care Proxy or a Health Care Proxy without a Living Will. If you do have a Living Will, however, failing to name a Health Care Representative may make it difficult to ensure that your Living Will wishes are carried out because no one will be acting on your behalf.

Medical Mumbo Jumbo

Advance Directive for Health Care—A combination Living Will and Health Care Proxy that outlines your wishes at the end of life and also appoints a Health Care Representative to act on your behalf if you are unable to make your own medical decisions; also called a *Health Care Advance Directive*.

Health Care Proxy—A legal document appointing a Health Care Representative to make your medical decisions if you can't; also called a *Durable Power of Attorney for Health Care, Advance Directive for Health Care—Proxy Directive, Medical Power of Attorney*, and *Advance Directive for Health Care*.

> **Living Will**—A legal document that outlines your wishes regarding your medical care at the end of life, including treatments you want or don't want; also called an *Advance Directive for Health Care—Instruction Directive, Medical Directive,* or *Directive to Physicians.*

You've probably noticed that every time you visit a new physician, you're required to sign a statement that you've been told about that office's privacy policy. You can thank the Health Insurance Portability and Accountability Act (HIPAA) and its Privacy Rule for this additional paperwork. HIPAA prevents health care providers from releasing your health care information to anyone, unless you've specifically stated, in writing, who can receive this information. That means that no longer will we have made-for-TV movie moments when the surgeon comes into the waiting room to deliver the good or bad news to the waiting family. Instead, the results of your surgery, for example, can only be given to your Health Care Representative. As with all laws and rules, HIPAA has pros and cons. On the one hand, it prevents people you don't want to know your medical condition from learning private information about you (for example, an estranged child or separated husband). But, on the other hand, it may keep the people you want to know about your care and to make decisions for you from learning about what ails you. That's why it's so important to specifically state, in writing, who you want to learn about your medical conditions and to make decisions for you if you are unable. This is your Health Care Representative.

If you have the ability to make your own medical decision, it remains your decision to make. Your Health Care Representative only makes decisions for you if you can't make decisions for yourself. Your inability to make decisions can be permanent or temporary, which is why it's important to have a Health Care Proxy in place today. Temporary incapacity may result from drug-induced confusion, high levels of painkillers, or anesthesia. Permanent incapacity can be from illness or injury. As with your other fiduciaries, you don't need to name a medical expert to serve as your Health Care Representative. Instead, you need to name the individual or individuals who can ask the right questions and exercise sound judgment. Most of all, you need a Health Care Representative who will implement your wishes for end of life care pursuant to your Living Will.

Your Health Care Proxy should outline not only who can act on your behalf, but also what your Health Care Representative can and cannot do on your behalf. In addition to making medical decisions, your Health Care Representative should also be able to review your medical records, talk to your doctors, and obtain different care or second opinions. Talk to your counselor for more information about the powers allowed to a Health Care Representative in your state.

Your Health Care Representative is charged with following your wishes for end of life care. But, as noted above, a simple statement such as, "Don't keep me hooked up to machines," isn't enough. That's why it's important to have a Living Will that outlines, in writing and according to the laws of your state, the exact medical care you want or don't want—and the situations in which your wishes should be followed.

What Does All This Medical Stuff Mean?

Most individuals state in their Advance Directive or Living Will that they do not want to receive medical treatment in certain situations. It's important to understand what exactly it is you're refusing. Thanks to Shawn D. Glisson, MD, FACP, my coauthor of *Wants, Wishes, and Wills: A Medical and Legal Guide to Protecting Yourself and Your Family in Sickness and in Health* (Financial Times Press, May 2007) the following is a brief review of the medical stuff you may choose to refuse (if you want more details, check the Glossary):

Antibiotics—Drugs designed to fight infections.

Artificially administered feeding and fluids— Nutrition and hydration provided to a person who cannot eat or drink on his or her own.

Cardiopulmonary Resuscitation (CPR)—Rescue breathing and chest compressions used to keep a heart beating.

Defibrillation—Using an electronic device to shock a heart back to its normal rhythm or to restart a heart.

Respiratory Support—Giving a patient who cannot breathe on his or her own oxygen through a variety of different methods.

Surgery—Any procedure or operation.

Most women I talk to are adamant that they be allowed to die with grace and dignity, and not hooked up to, as they put it, "lots of machines." Your Living Will should specify the situations in which the document should take effect, for example, if you're permanently unconscious, in the last stages of a **terminal health condition**, gravely injured, or otherwise unlikely to survive your current medical condition. If one of these conditions exists, your Living Will should state the medical care you want or don't want, such as cardiopulmonary resuscitation, ventilation, and feeding tubes and fluids. Your Living Will should contain your preference if you are pregnant. The choices could include being kept alive until a reasonable certainty exists that a healthy child would be born or providing that your Living Will take effect regardless of whether you are pregnant. You may also want to include a provision if you wish to be an organ donor. Please note that a Living Will is not a *Do Not Resuscitate Order* or *DNR* Order. Only a licensed physician, often after consultation with the patient or the patient's Health Care Representative and with consideration given to the patient's Living Will, if any, can issue a DNR Order.

When you're thinking about the terms of your Living Will and treatment you want or don't want, ask yourself the following questions: If you're suffering from advanced dementia and are otherwise healthy, do you want to refuse all further health care? If the use of a ventilator or respirator for a brief period of time during a chronic illness could return you to an active and healthy lifestyle, do you want to emphatically refuse such treatment? Are you adamant that you do not wish to receive artificially administered nutrition and hydration? Answers to these questions should all be outlined in your Living Will, with as much detail as you are able to provide.

Your Living Will should be drafted by an attorney and contain your specific wants and wishes. A form you've printed off the Internet or a boilerplate document given to you by the staff of the local hospital when you're being admitted isn't going to reflect your particular health and circumstances. Include any religious preferences you have in your Living Will. The Roman Catholic Church, for example, offers suggested language that states the Catholic definition of life as well as a request that the Sacraments of Reconciliation and the Anointing of the Sick and Viaticum be provided. Talk to your priest, rabbi, cleric, pastor, or other religious advisor for appropriate language for your faith. Share this language with your lawyer and ask that it be included in your Living Will. Take the opportunity to create an advance directive that reflects exactly what medical care and treatment you want or don't want at the end of life.

Although it doesn't happen often, a Living Will can request that your physicians and your Health Care Representative take all actions necessary to prolong your life. That means that you want to be kept alive and that all means necessary should be tried in order to fulfill your wishes. As with everything throughout the book, this is your decision. What's important is that you provide both your health care providers and your Health Care Representative with a clear, written directive of your intentions regarding your medical care. It's important to note, again, that the final decision remains yours, so long as you're able to make such decisions. If you're unable to make your own decisions, the decision belongs to your Health Care Representative with due regard to your wishes as outlined in your Living Will.

Living Will Language

Every state has its own statutory Living Will language. In addition, you should consider the following directives:

1. Avoid vague and general statements such as "extraordinary means" or "heroic measures."

2. Outline the scenarios in which your Living Will should become effective. Examples include if you're suffering from irreversible advanced dementia, you're in a persistent vegetative state with irreversible brain damage or in an irreversible coma, you've received a terminal prognosis, or there is no expectation of recovery.

3. Include a specific list of the medical care you don't want to receive or have continued, such as respiratory assistance, therapeutic treatments, or cardiopulmonary resuscitation.

4. Specifically state that you want or don't want intravenous feeding and fluids.

5. Include a statement that you wish to be an organ donor, if feasible, and that all steps should be taken to make your organs available. Of course, if you don't want to be an organ donor, do not include this statement.

6. State your wishes if you are pregnant. For example, you could choose to be kept alive as a human incubator if a child will be born, regardless of the child's prognosis, or only if a medical certainty exists that a non-disabled child will be born. Alternatively, you can request that your

Living Will be given full force and effect whether or not you're expecting—in other words, you won't be kept alive just because you're pregnant.

Document Review

Once you've made all of your important decisions and your documents are drafted, be sure to sign at least four duplicate originals of each of your Health Care Proxy, Living Will, and Power of Attorney. Because original documents can be lost or destroyed, keep one duplicate original at your lawyer's office so at least one original remains safe. Tell your Health Care Representative and Agent where the other original documents are located. I call this location the important paper drawer and talk more about it in Chapter 9 ("Is There Anything Else You Should Do to Be Prepared?"). In the event of a medical emergency, you want your representative to have immediate access to the necessary documents. In addition, you should tell your primary care physician that you have signed the documents and ask if he or she would like a copy. When you are admitted to a hospital, bring along a copy yourself.

Most important, if you can, hold on to your original documents!!! Tell your Agent and Health Care Representative to do the same. Ask your financial institutions and providers to make copies and to return the originals to you. Why? Once you've given all of your original documents away, it will be next to impossible to get them back. If you do become incapacitated and unable to sign new documents, it's as if you never went to the trouble of signing the documents in the first place.

All of us hate the idea of losing our independence and our ability to act for ourselves. So we avoid the issue. However, as an aging population, we can't avoid tackling these tough issues any longer. I know that all I've done is lecture you throughout this book to get your plans in place; but it's the only way I know to encourage you to act. I'm particularly passionate about the need for Powers of Attorney, Living Wills and Health Care Proxies. You'll help your loved ones make tough decisions if you tell them what you want. You'll also help yourself by having the individuals you want in place to make those decisions. These are difficult subjects. I know—I deal with them every day. Think of it like your yearly mammogram. You don't like it, but you do it for yourself and your loved ones. Think of this the same way, with one added benefit. Once it's done, you won't need to think about it for years!

What Should You Do Next?

1. Sign a general durable Power of Attorney naming an Agent and successor Agents.

2. Outline your end of life care wishes in a Living Will.

3. Name a Health Care Representative and successors in a Health Care Proxy.

Chapter 9

Is There Anything Else You Should Do to Be Prepared?

YES!!!!!!!! Estate planning isn't just about writing a Will, locking it up in a vault, and forgetting about it. You can continue to assist your loved ones by not only regularly reviewing your legal and financial plan, but also by pointing them in the right direction when the inevitable happens.

How Often Should You Look at Your Estate Planning Documents?

I recommend reviewing your documents every five years, or whenever you experience a major life change event or a significant increase or decrease in assets. A major life change can be a birth, death, divorce, bankruptcy, disability, or a change in your health. As far as a big change in your net worth, let's just say that your lawyer is the first person you should call when you win the lottery!

The Important Paper Drawer

Every time I head out on a long trip, I remind my sister that everything she needs if I "buy the farm" when I'm away can be found in my "important paper drawer." Most of you probably already have a drawer or file cabinet where the important stuff can be found and have told someone that this is the place to look if something bad happens. If you don't, it's high time for you to find a space to collect and store what your loved ones need. A terrific alternative to a drawer is a firebox. I have had many relatives affected by hurricanes and fires, so having everything important in one location has made for fast evacuations or peace of mind when it was impossible to reach the firebox in time.

I have a red notebook in my desk with personal information, which my children know about. I have created a Word document on our computer where I write my funeral plans, location of our safe deposit box, etc.
—Lillian, age 60

Perhaps you're thinking, I don't need a firebox, I have a safe deposit box. The problem with a safe deposit box for important papers is that it may be difficult for your loved ones to access a safe deposit box in the event of an emergency. This is especially true with regard to Powers of Attorney and health care documents. For example, if you're injured on the Friday evening of a holiday weekend, your loved ones may not have access to the bank until the following Tuesday to obtain the necessary legal documents. Or worse, they may lack the legal authority to enter the box, making it impossible to help you in a time of need. That's why having the documents in an easily accessible location, and telling your loved ones where that location is, is so important.

Letters of Instruction

One of the most helpful things you can leave for your loved ones in your important paper drawer, in addition to your funeral plans, is a Letter of Instruction. This is a letter or memorandum that serves as a road map to everything they need to know. I'm continually impressed by the thoughtfulness of both family members and clients who take the time to put this information together. The headaches and heartaches you prevent are countless.

Begin your Letter of Instruction with a list of who should be contacted on your passing. In addition to your professional advisors (your attorney, accountant, and financial advisor), write down the family members and friends who should be notified. Include phone numbers and addresses. In a time of crisis and mourning, your loved ones may forget to call your high school pals or your former business partners. Point them in the right direction.

I leave a note for my husband every time I travel on business that outlines where all the important documents are. I also leave him a contact at my place of business who can help him navigate through all of my benefits/insurance/pension, etc. I do this frequently because he can't seem to remember where we keep the forks after seven years of marriage, so I feel the need to leave him a little "map" in the event of a disaster. Hopefully, hearing it every month will help him shift to "auto-pilot" should he ever need to! I have also told him not to throw away my designer shoes and bags because he wouldn't know Louis Vuitton from K-mart.

—Mimi, age 39

Next, get down to business and outline where everything can be found. Here's what they'll be looking for:

1. Your original Last Will and Testament and other legal documents, including deeds, Trust agreements, original stock certificates, cemetery plot records, and titles to vehicles, boats, and other titled assets.

2. Income and gift tax returns.

3. Your safe deposit box and key.

4. Bank and brokerage accounts and account numbers.

5. Life insurance and annuity policies, policy numbers, and whereabouts of the original policies.

6. Organizations that may provide a death benefit, such as unions, the Veteran's Administration, and social organizations.

7. Available employee and death benefits and your human resources contact information.

8. Other assets you own or are entitled to.

9. List of debts and payments that may be due.

10. Location of all account passwords or other access information, including your online service provider. (It's incredibly difficult to cancel online accounts without a password.)

11. Location of any hidden items. This might include jewelry, sterling silver, or cash. Give your heirs a hint where to look.

While your loved ones still have to clean out your closet and your nightstand drawer, save them the task of having to look everywhere for the important documents. The more organized you are and the more detailed your Letter of Instruction, the easier it will be for your Executor to begin the **estate administration** process. This won't be fun for them; but more information equals fewer headaches. When you're mourning the death of a loved one, you already have enough pain.

Funeral Planning

When I first thought about funeral planning, I decided to call my dentist. Comparing the two, the dentist sounded like much more fun. Then I thought about it some more. I've attend the funerals of friends, family, colleagues, and clients. Each has moved me in different ways. There have also been aspects that I didn't care for—simply because they didn't reflect my style and values. This made me realize how helpful it is to families when their loved one leaves them guidelines for their own life celebration.

> *I have verbally told those around me some specifics like a closed casket (no one will get my hair and make-up right!) and no bra (or I will come back and haunt them).*
> —Gabriella, age 39

Many of you may have already selected a funeral home and the details of your service, and prepaid these services. I'll thank you on behalf of your loved ones. It's a great thing to do. If you have done this, be sure to leave the details so there's no confusion when the services are needed. If you haven't, give some consideration to exactly what it is you'd like. Is it a full funeral service, or perhaps a low-key memorial service or life celebration? It's best not to include this information in your Last Will and Testament, because these decisions are often made before the lawyer is contacted and your testamentary documents read.

Funeral Facts

Leaving your loves ones the following funeral facts is incredibly helpful. Don't be shy, if something is important to you, let them know.

1. If funeral plans have been made and/or paid for, provide the name and contact information for the Funeral Director.

2. List your wishes regarding burial or cremation. Include information regarding the location of a cemetery plot or mausoleum. If you've requested cremation, include details regarding the final disposition of your ashes. Provide the location of any legal documents that include additional requests. The Veteran's Administration provides many burial benefits, so remind your loved ones if you served your country as a soldier, sailor, or other serviceperson.

3. Outline whether you prefer a full religious funeral celebration or a simple memorial service. Details regarding the actual service, readings, speakers, music, and officiants are very beneficial.

4. Discuss your preferences regarding visitation and whether your casket should be open or closed. Include details about what you'd like to wear or objects that should be placed in the casket (such as photographs, religious items, jewelry, or mementos).

5. Name the charitable organization or organizations to receive donations in lieu of flowers.

---

6. Provide the names of individuals you would like to have serve as pallbearers.

7. Give your suggestions for a post-funeral gathering, whether that gathering is a simple lunch or a big party celebrating you.

8. Include a reminder to your loved ones to have a trusted friend or employee stay at your home during the funeral and post-funeral gathering. There are many thieves who make it a practice to review funeral notices to find out when homes will be empty and a good target for a break-in.

In addition to your funeral desires, it's helpful to leave some details regarding your obituary and the publications in which your obituary should be printed. Generally, an obituary outlines your loved ones—those living and those who have passed before you—your education and employment history, military service, accomplishments, prizes and honors, and places of residence. Instead of looking at this as a sad task, consider it an opportunity for rediscovery of your life. Celebrate your accomplishments while you're at it. Your loved ones will appreciate the reminder of everything you've done.

The end of life isn't the glamorous ending we see in movies. Unfortunately, films forget to show the mountains of paperwork and tax returns that await the survivors. Some planning and letters won't change this, but it will make the next steps for your family and friends a little less difficult. And that's a good thing.

What Should You Do Next?

1. Identify your important paper drawer or purchase a firebox. Let your loved ones know where to look.

2. Prepare your Letter of Instruction. Be as detailed as you can be—the more information you provide, the more instruction you give.

3. Outline your funeral wishes.

Chapter 10

How Do You Talk to Your Loved Ones About Your Death?

There is nothing pleasant about death or conversing about death. It's painful and emotional to talk about the death of anyone, let alone our loved ones. But it's an important subject and one you shouldn't put off discussing.

One reason it's critical to sit down and confer about these issues is that it keeps your loved ones from scratching their heads and wondering what Mom would have wanted, whether the question relates to your health care, your finances, or your funeral. I could give you countless examples of loved one's ashes sitting in the back of a bedroom closet, sometimes for a decade, while the family decides what should be done with those ashes. As I always say, I don't think the closet would have been Mom's choice.

Having these discussions also eliminates strife between your loved ones when they all believe you want something different. There is nothing sadder to me than children fighting over the care a family member's wants or needs. For example: Should Grandma be at home or in a nursing facility? Did she want life support or not?

An even worse situation is when I'm called to visit Dad in the nursing home to see if he wants a public funeral or a private, simple service. Really, loved ones should be able to come to some agreement on these issues and not involve counsel. But sadly, there are many children who find the illness or death of a parent as an opportunity to act out on every perceived lifetime slight. Don't even get me started on the family bullies who berate, yell, and scream until they get their way, even if it's not what their loved one wants. It's pathetic; I agree—but it happens more than you'll ever know. That's why it's imperative to take charge and make it clear to one and all exactly what it is you want.

While your wishes should be in writing (for example, in your health care documents or Letter of Instruction), having a verbal conversation is also very helpful to your loved ones. As Virginia Morris wrote in *Talking About Death Won't Kill You*, "Have you ever really imagined what it is like to make life-and death decisions for someone whom you can't live without?" Explaining what you want, face-to-face, will help your loved ones truly understand what it is you want and that any actions they take on your behalf are what you would have done for yourself. You may be asking your Health Care Representative to make incredibly difficult decisions. Assure him or her that it's what you want and that there should be no feelings of guilt in making the decisions. Your loved ones will be able to think back on your conversations and act knowing that truly, these were your wishes. Julia, age 42, wishes her grandmother had told her what she wanted, instead of simply saying that she had a Living Will in a drawer in her bedroom. "When Nana slumped over during lunch, I panicked and called 911. Watching the paramedics pound on her frail, 92-year-old body, I knew I'd made a huge mistake, that this was the last thing she wanted. Making that call is one of the biggest regrets of my life."

The most difficult part of having these discussions is starting the conversation. There is no easy segue from, "Honey, how was your day?" to, "I've been thinking about my funeral; this is what I would like." I always suggest that clients blame it on me and begin the conversation with, "I had a meeting with my lawyer last week. She thought it would be a good idea to outline our discussions." You can then roll right into the subject.

Depending upon the emotional state of your husband, significant other, or children, it may be best to give them a heads up that the discussion is coming. For example, let them know that you'd like to have a family meeting to discuss your thoughts and concerns as you get older. Often, it's beneficial to avoid using the word *death*, and instead use phrases such as "sharing responsibility" or "outlining my wishes." If your loved ones shut you out and refuse to discuss the issues, don't be ashamed to resort to trickery. A long car ride is the perfect opportunity to bombard your passengers with your thoughts. If they act like two year olds and put their hands over their ears and start yelling "No, no, no," treat them like two year olds and keep repeating your message. Eventually it will sink in.

Don't Worry Honey, I'll Take Care of Everything

Hmmm...we've all heard that one before. Last time I checked, the garbage still hadn't been taken out. As much as you love your significant other, he or she can't do your estate planning for you. Only you can sign your Will and Trust and distribute your own assets. No one can do it for you. As far as your estate planning goes, you can't rely on anyone but yourself.

What you tell your loved ones and what you don't is up to you. Sharing your thoughts for end of life care is, in my opinion, critical for the reasons I've outlined. Make sure your named Health Care Representative and Agent will agree to take on this role. It's always wise to check with the Guardians you've identified to make sure they're able to serve. Taking care of someone else's little ones is a big responsibility; and sadly, not everyone is up to the task.

As for sharing the details of your actual estate plan, that really depends on you, your relationship with your loved ones, and your plan. Most families have open relationships and don't hide anything. If that describes your inner circle, go ahead and share the details of your plan. Others depend on children, siblings, or others for advice. Let them in on your decisions; they may be able to help you with future planning issues.

Unfortunately, there are many women who are bullied by husbands and children who demand certain treatment or knowledge. If this is your situation, I say don't tell them anything. They have no need to know. It isn't their business until you're gone. I can't say it enough: The people you select to act for you and what you want to have happen when you die is your decision and your decision alone. It isn't about what someone else wants, expects, or anticipates. It also isn't about what you think you should do. Do what you want and how you want it done. Your daughter might be really angry that you've created a Trust for her benefit. So why tell her now? You'll only have to listen to her whine and complain. You are her mother. You *do* know what's best. So do exactly what you think is best. If you're concerned that someone's nose will be really out of joint when he or she learns your decisions, leave a letter of explanation along with your Will. Outline why you picked Abigail to serve instead of Anna. You had a reason when you made your decision; share it if you think it will help, but don't feel obligated to do so.

One of the benefits to sharing your estate planning with your family and friends is your ability to encourage them to think about putting their own affairs in order. Brag that you finally got your documents completed. Flaunt your new-found knowledge at a family gathering or cocktail party. Ask them if they have questions now that you're a know-it-all on what's important. Offer to recommend an ace attorney. Even if they don't ask questions, share your thoughts on the subject. As you know from reading this book, planning is critically important, especially when it comes to health care documents and Powers of Attorney. If you get just one person to take these documents seriously, you will have accomplished something really terrific.

As I've noted throughout this book, I'm a control kind of gal. If you're reading this book, my guess is that you are, too. You've taken control of your planning and affairs (or at least you're on your way to doing just that). Be sure to follow through on your control by discussing these issues and your wants with your loved ones.

What Should You Do Next?

1. Explain to your friends and family the end of life care you want and expect. Keep telling them until it sinks in!

2. Put your plans in place—not those demanded of you by loved ones.

3. Share the details of your planning if it is appropriate in your situation.

Chapter 11

What Should You Do in Special Situations?

As we grow older, our goals change. So do our situations and needs. The plan that works for you as a successful single is not necessarily the same plan that you'll want 10, 20, or even 30 years later. It's wise to review your plan every five years or whenever you experience a major life change, such as a death in the family, divorce, birth of a child, change in residence or (my favorite!) a large increase in your net worth.

Not only will your situations change, each of you reading this book is very likely in a very different situation. Here are a few considerations for each of you, no matter who you are or where you are in your life. Remember, because things change, so can your estate plan!

Successful Singles

You've worked your tail off. Maybe you've started your own business or broken the glass ceiling. Or, perhaps you've studied hard and are now a talented physician or professor. No matter what you do, you're doing great, and your bank accounts show it. Of course, you can just leave all to chance and make no plan. But what if your wealth passes to your parents who don't need it, only to be taxed when you die and again when they do? Maybe you'd rather take care of your nieces, nephews, or a favorite cousin. Or maybe you want half to go to your alma mater and half to the local hospital. Be clear and put it in writing. Let's not forget how important it is to line up friends or family members to help you out if you can't act for yourself. I'm single, and I've asked my sister to help out. If she can't do it for any reason, my cousin has agreed to stand-in when important decisions need to be made. Not only do I appreciate their help, I feel better knowing that this burden, if it arises, won't fall on my mom and dad.

Homemakers

Let's face it, you've worked hard too—harder than your husband probably gives you credit for. (Am I right?) Even though the dollars in your bank account may have come from your husband's hard work, his hard work was enhanced by everything you did. Just because only one of you receives a W-2 at tax time doesn't mean that you both don't need to plan. First and foremost, you need to talk to your husband. You need to have assets in your name alone to use your applicable exclusion from estate tax. These can be outright assets or assets owned as tenants-in-common instead of as joint tenants. You also need to harp on your husband to think about these issues. Confirm that his plans, if he has any, provide for you. Be sure his 401(k) and IRA are designated correctly so you receive the benefit; and, if you're not alive, your children do. Make sure you both have Powers of Attorney, Health Care Proxies, and Living Wills in case of illness or injury. You need to act as a team to tackle the unthinkable, not only for your benefit, but also for your family.

Widows

It's not easy transitioning from marriage to widowhood. Perhaps you hadn't signed a check in decades. Or maybe you were too busy caring for an ailing husband to worry about life's details. Now that you're alone, it's time to think of yourself. First and foremost, after your husband's death, review your Power of Attorney and Health Care Proxy. Be sure you have successors named. If not, call your counselor as soon as possible to be sure you have up-to-date documents. Review your husband's Will or Trust. Did he set up a Trust for you? If so, do you have a Power of Appointment over the Trust assets? Talk to your lawyer to see if you should exercise this power. Review your own assets. You may now have significantly more than you'd planned for. Consider your options and your goals. They may have changed. Be sure the plan you currently have in place works with your new situation.

Generous Grandmothers

We already know you dote on your grandkids—that's your job! You're in a unique position, as a generous grandmother, to do more than just dote. You can pay tuition expenses and medical bills. You can make gifts using Trusts, UTMA or UGMA accounts, or Section

529 plans. You can provide for your grandchildren's education for decades to come with education Trusts or generation skipping Trusts. The opportunities are countless to spoil your loved ones for years.

Divorcées

You were probably wondering why, in Chapter 6 ("What's a Will? What's a Trust? How Do You Use Them to Put Your Plan in Place?") I recommended that you bring a copy of the Property Settlement Agreement to your initial meeting with your lawyer. It's important because, under the terms of that Agreement, you may have certain obligations that impact your planning. For example, you may be required to maintain an insurance policy for the benefit of your former honey. If this is the case, your lawyer may inquire as to whether that policy can be placed into an Irrevocable Life Insurance Trust to reduce taxes due at your death. Or, you may also be paying your ex alimony and be required to leave him a set dollar amount in case you die while you're still shelling out.

If you have small children, you need to name a Guardian for your kids in case you die while they're minors and their father has already died or can't serve. Yes, it's unlikely that you and your ex-significant other would kick the bucket at the same time; but, you could die within days of each other. Be sure you have the Guardian you want named.

It's also important to remember the laws of intestacy that are on the books in some states. In case you've forgotten, if you have no living relatives, your assets could pass to your step-children. That's right, your ex-husband's kids—the ones that never spoke to you during Thanksgiving dinner and in many ways made your life a living hell. For many of you, you'd rather see Leona Helmsley's dog get your assets. You can keep this from happening by having a Will or Trust that outlines exactly what you want.

Cohabiters

You're shacking up. It's romantic, sharing a nest without any of the complications that married life can bring. No matter how many candlelit dinners and vacations you and your partner take, no matter how happy you are, if one of you gets sick or dies, there are no laws to protect you unless you've planned accordingly. Let's say you're injured, unless you've named your boyfriend as your Health Care Representative, he can't make health care decisions for you—even though you spent hours telling him what you wanted. Without a Power of Attorney, he can't pay your bills or do anything on your behalf. If you're so ill a Guardian is needed, the court may look at your blood relatives first to serve for you. Maybe that's what you'd prefer, but because you didn't put anything in writing, no one will ever know, will they?

Then of course, there's the disaster when you die. Besides the grief, there are likely to be disagreements over what belonged to you and what belonged to him. Remember, you're not there to remind your family that the TV belongs to Ted. If Ted can't prove it, well, it just leaves a big mess. Most of all, without a Will or Trust that provides for Ted, he'll receive nothing from your estate. It will pass to your relatives, no matter how remote they are. While we'd like to think that our families would do the right thing and help Ted out, there's no requirement that that take place. When you live together, you need to plan for both the good times and the bad.

Lesbians

For single lesbians, the recommendations for the successful single apply to you. If you're currently in a relationship and want your partner to be your beneficiary, think of yourself as a cohabiter. You need to have the necessary documents in place so your girlfriend can make health care and financial decisions for you. If you want to take care of her for life, you need to be sure that she's the beneficiary of your estate or the beneficiary of a Trust you might set up for her benefit. Because there are no federal tax benefits available to married gay couples, tax planning becomes very important. Lifetime gifting may be the best thing for your loved one.

Caregivers

While this book is directed at your planning, no doubt many of you are thinking of loved ones as you turn each page. The role of today's caregiver isn't easy. How do you suggest to an older loved one that her memory is slipping and it's time to put her affairs in order? As difficult as it is to raise the subject, you all benefit from doing so. Here's what I recommend (and have used with my loved ones!):

1. **We're getting organized!** Try saying this: "Mom and Dad (insert name of older relative here), I'm getting my documents in order. You both need to as well. Let's get organized together."

2. **I'm the bossy b*&^%; this is what we're doing!** Sometimes playing hardball is the only way to go. Sadly, I know this firsthand. They won't like it, but you'd make them go to the doctor, right? Consider a trip to the lawyer no different than a trip to the cardiologist.

3. **It's free!** While this might not be true—and will require you to pay the bill—it's amazing how interested older folks are in an estate plan that costs nothing. Tell your aunt you won the estate planning at a charity lunch. Explain to your uncle that your lawyer friend is doing you a favor. Sure, it's a fib, but if it works....

Heiresses

Yes, you know who you are—lots of silver spoons and all that? Probably not. But many women have been fortunate enough to have very successful loved ones and have never wanted for anything (and yet we don't act like Paris Hilton...interesting). We're the beneficiaries of Trusts and family wealth that come with responsibilities. It's important to understand what powers you have as a beneficiary. Can you direct who receives the assets when you die (a Power of Appointment)? Can you use the Trust proceeds during life for the benefit of another (a Lifetime Limited Power of Appointment)? Will the Trust assets be included in your estate for estate tax purposes? The more you know, the better you can plan. Review Trust agreements. Ask questions. Learn your responsibilities.

As you know by now, no matter what situation describes you, you need to get out there and plan! Plan for yourself, plan for your loved ones, plan for your bottom line. Because you are all unique, it's also very important not to listen to the war stories and tales of woe from your friends or the ladies in your book club, office, or support group. What applies to them almost certainly doesn't apply to you. You need your own individualized estate plan. Whatever it is that inspires you, be inspired and start planning.

What Should You Do Next?

1. Identify your unique situation.
2. Review documents related to your situation (cohabitation, Trust, and property settlement agreements, for example).

Chapter 12

What Happens If You Are Appointed as a Fiduciary?

Just as you've been considering your estate planning and the care of your loved ones, young and old, so have your friends and family. You've identified them to act for you as Executors, Trustees, and Guardians. It's likely they've identified you as well. So what happens when you're called upon to serve? Here are a few things you should know—and do.

First, being nominated or appointed as a fiduciary doesn't mean you have to take on the job. You are always given the power to renounce, or say no thank you, to your appointment. It's much wiser to pass than be saddled with responsibilities that you just can't handle. Many of the fiduciary litigations we see involve Executors or Trustees who don't do anything. If you've got too much on your plate or just aren't up to the challenge, say so. There is nothing wrong with saying, "No."

Alternatively, if you're concerned that at some time in the future you may need to step aside, review the document nominating you to be sure you have the power to resign. While it should seem obvious that you can, not all documents include this provision. If there is no power to resign, a court proceeding will be required to discharge you from your responsibilities. Some Trusts can last for decades, so find out now if you're concerned about your ability to step down in the future. I know that I certainly don't want to be administering my nephew's Trust at age 86!

A fiduciary is a position of trust. You are required to follow the terms of the Will or Trust that has named you for the benefit of the beneficiaries. Your duty also requires you to balance the competing interests of both the current and future beneficiaries. In many ways, as a fiduciary, you're much like a small business owner. You have the responsibility of managing a taxable entity with specific goals and requirements.

Before You Do Anything, Ask Questions!

The most important piece of advice I give to any client when a loved one dies is not to do anything. Allow yourself time to grieve. Attend the funeral or memorial service. Then sit down and learn what happens next. The biggest problems we see result when family members or fiduciaries run out and cash in savings bonds, rollover IRAs, or otherwise move assets around in such a way that a carefully crafted estate plan is destroyed...often with dire tax consequences.

As the newly-appointed CEO of Estate A or Trust B, make an appointment with the attorney representing the entity. Be sure you have a rapport and confidence in him or her. If not, feel free to find new counsel to represent you. You're in charge and should find professionals you believe in to assist you. Ask for specific timelines of required tasks (such as filing tax returns or filing status reports with the court). Request a checklist of other requirements or suggestions. Inquire as to what you can do and what the lawyer or accountant does. Make a determination as to what you'll be doing and what they'll be doing. Remember, just because you have an attorney assisting you it doesn't mean you can sit back and relax. It's your responsibility to keep after your counselor and accountant to be sure that they're doing what they've said they'd do. Refer back to the key dates they've provided and keep after them!

Key Tax Dates

For Trusts, income tax returns (Forms 1041) are due on April 15th, just like every other taxpayer. If a Trust is a split-interest Trust or a private foundation Trust, different returns may be due. Check with your tax preparer for specifics.

For estates, income tax returns (Forms 1041) for the estate are due on the 15th day of the third month after the end of the fiscal year. That's right, like a business, an estate can choose a fiscal year for tax reporting purposes. There are many advantages to this, which should be discussed with your accountant or attorney. And, let's not forget the last income tax return for the **Decedent**, which is the Executor's responsibility (due April 15th the year after death).

The Executor is also responsible for ensuring that any gift tax returns (IRS Form 709) not filed for the Decedent during his or her life are prepared and filed. This return is due on April 15th on the year following the death of the Decedent. The federal estate tax return (IRS Form 706) is due nine months after the date of death of the Decedent. The due dates for state estate and inheritance tax returns vary...check with your lawyer or CPA for details.

Are you already thinking twice about taking on the taxing job of a fiduciary?

Getting to know the estate or Trust beneficiaries is also wise. Trusts for minor children often come with a great deal of discretion. Learn from a child's parent or Guardian if the child has any special needs. Understand what is needed to assist with the child's education or other support. You may be called upon to make tough decisions; knowing who you are making decisions for is always beneficial.

It's also critical to keep detailed records, just as you would for any business. Record all income received and the source. Retain receipts for all expenditures, no matter how big or small. This makes it clear that you have acted appropriately in your administration of any estate or Trust. Also pay attention to all investments. A fiduciary should maintain, if possible, a diversified portfolio of assets. No one wants to be the Trustee who only had shares of Enron in the Trust's brokerage account. If financial management isn't your thing, talk to a portfolio expert or other financial guru. Explain the purposes of the Trust or estate, any liquidity needs (such as large tax payments), and goals for distribution. Ask for help if you need it.

How Does the Funeral Home Get Paid?

Funeral homes are businesses, just like any other. They want and need to get paid. But unlike most businesses, they understand what happens at death. Particularly, funeral homes know that a Power of Attorney is no longer effective on the death of the Principal. However, the number of times funeral homes encourage loved ones to just "write a check" from the account of a deceased loved one using a Power of Attorney is countless. Be clear that the funeral home will be paid as soon as the estate account is opened and funds are available. You, as the fiduciary, are not personally responsible for paying the funeral home bill or any bills of the estate for that matter.

Generally, the job of an Executor is more intensive and time-consuming than that of a Trustee. As an Executor, you are required to marshal (or collect) the estate assets. This may require you to clean up homes and sell real estate, dispose of personal property, and hunt down missing stock certificates. You'll also be required to obtain date of death valuations for all of the estate's assets. Sometimes it's the little things that take the most time: canceling credit cards, having the Decedent's mail forwarded, uncovering death benefits from social organizations, searching for a safe deposit box key, or wading through 50 years of junk in the basement. As one of my clients put it, "All of this paperwork is certainly taking my mind off my brother's death...but not in a good way."

Does a Fiduciary Get a Paycheck?

Yes! When you serve as an Executor, Trustee, or Guardian, you are entitled to commissions. The statues of the state in which the Decedent lived outline the commissions you are entitled to. These jobs are hard, so don't be shy about being paid for your hard work. If you don't want to take commissions, no one will object if you say, "No thank you." However, at the very least, you should be reimbursed for any out of pocket expenses. Keep detailed records of money you've spent on travel, postage, cleaning supplies, and anything else. These are tax deductible expenses of the estate or Trust—there's no reason you should paying these expenses yourself.

The job of fiduciary takes organization and diligence. You need to know what is required of you, the time frame for completing your responsibilities, and the beneficiaries you'll be assisting. In many ways, serving as a fiduciary is a thankless job. But in others, it is a wonderful opportunity to ensure that the wishes of your loved one are being carried out. Your dedication and assistance are appreciated—more than you will ever know.

What Should You Do Next?

1. Don't do anything until you talk to the lawyer representing the estate or Trust!

2. Understand the parameters of your appointment. If you are a Trustee, review the Trust document. Ask questions if there is anything you don't understand.

3. Ask for help! Professionals are there to make your job easier. Good advisors will work with you, doing as much or as little as you would like.

4. Take commissions!

Conclusion

Estate Planning Checklist

Every day I speak with smart women like you about protecting their assets, as well as their other estate planning concerns, and what they should do next. I also surveyed ladies across the land for their feelings on the subject. The one thing everyone had in common was a request for a checklist of what to do and how to get started. While there are a few women who are frightened of the subject, most are anxious to put pen to paper. They want to do what they can today to be sure their families are taken care of and their wants satisfied if the unthinkable happens. So, instead of a call to get moving (you're already doing that if you're reading this—congratulations!), here's a checklist to keep you moving forward.

ESTATE PLANNING CHECKLIST

1. Ask friends, family, colleagues, and professional advisors to recommend an estate planning attorney. Alternatively, visit the Lawyer Locator Web sites listed in "Suggested Resources" to search for counsel in your state. Select an attorney who works in your state of residence and specializes in estate planning.

2. Make an appointment with the lawyer you've located. Be sure the appointment date works with your schedule. If you have health problems, surgeries scheduled, or a trip planned, ask the attorney if the necessary documents can be prepared to meet your timeline.

3. Prepare your Net Worth Statement:

NET WORTH STATEMENT

Asset	Ownership/ Beneficiary Designation	Current Value
Real Property		
Main Residence		
Vacation Home		
Time Share		
Business/Rental Property		
Vacant or Farm Land		
Other		
Personal Property		
Jewelry		
Antiques		
Sterling Silver		
Collections		
Artwork		

Asset	Ownership/ Beneficiary Designation	Current Value
Personal Property		
Equipment		
Automobiles		
Boats		
Motor Homes		
Other		
Intangible Personal Property		
Stock		
Bonds		
Brokerage Accounts		
Bank Accounts		
Certificates of Deposit		
Annuities		
Business Interests		
Partnerships		
Patents		
Copyrights		
Individual Retirement Accounts		
401(k) or 403(b) Accounts		
Other Retirement Benefits		
Stock Options		
Other Employee Benefit Items		

Trust Information

Include the names of any Trusts of which you are a beneficiary. If you have a copy of the Trust Agreement or Trust terms, attach a copy to your Net Worth Statement.

Life Insurance

Include the face value of each life insurance policy as well as the cash surrender value, if there is any.

Potential Inheritances

Make a list of potential inheritances. Your attorney will understand that this is simply a guess on your part, but any estimate may help evaluate your estate planning options for these and your other assets.

Liabilities

Mortgage Debt

Home Equity Line of Credit Debt

Credit Card Debt

Other Debt or Liabilities

4. Think about your estate planning goals and concerns. Do you want to provide for your children's education? Are you concerned about your partner's well-being if you die? Are there charitable organizations you want to benefit? Who should serve as your fiduciaries? Should your estate pay all the taxes or should each beneficiary pay his or her share of the taxes? If your counselor hasn't asked you to complete an estate planning questionnaire or information sheet, prepare the following information to bring to your initial meeting.

   A. Your full legal name and any aliases.

   B. Your legal address.

   C. Your social security number.

   D. Your citizenship.

   E. Your husband or domestic partner's full legal name (and aliases), address, citizenship, and social security number.

F. If you're widowed, your late husband's name and date of death.

G. If you're divorced, your former husband's name and divorce date. Also bring along a copy of any Property Settlement or similar agreement. This will help your lawyer determine if any additional planning is required by the document.

H. Name of your accountant, if any. Let your lawyer know if you would like your accountant to be involved in the planning process.

I. Name of your financial advisor, if any. Let your lawyer know if you would like your financial advisor to be involved in the planning process.

J. Any pre-nuptial or ante-nuptial agreements.

K. Names, addresses, and ages of your children, grandchildren, and all other beneficiaries. Include the relationship of each individual.

L. Names of your parents and any potential inheritances.

M. Your net worth statement. Include both your assets and your liabilities.

N. Bring copies of beneficiary designations for your life insurance, IRAs, 401(k)s, and any other asset that has such a designation.

O. If you're a beneficiary of any Trust, bring along a copy of the Trust Agreement if you have it. This includes any Trusts created by a late husband, parent, or grandparent.

P. Copies of any gift tax returns (IRS Form 709) you may have filed or copies of gift tax returns filed by a husband that you may have signed. If you haven't filed any gift tax returns, make a list of any big gifts or loans you may have made. Use $10,000 as the trigger point: Make a list of all transfers you've made of more than $10,000 or totaling more than $10,000 in any calendar year.

Q. A list of any specific or charitable bequests you'd like to make, for example, $1,000 to each grandchild or $10,000 to your alma mater. Provide exact legal names and addresses.

R. A brief summary of your estate planning goals. Your summary might say you'd like to provide for your significant other for life and then provide for your children. Or, maybe you want to skip one child and provide for your grandkids instead. Perhaps you're only interested in benefiting charitable organizations. Write down what you're thinking to help point your counselor (and you) in the right direction.

S. A list of your concerns and anything else that's important to you.

T. Names and addresses of the individuals to serve as your Executor or Personal Representative, Trustee, and Guardian, as well as at least two successors for each position.

U. Name of your Agent to serve under your Power of Attorney, as well as at least two successor Agents. Let your attorney know if you have concerns about your named Agent or the breadth of a General Durable Power of Attorney.

V. Name of your Health Care Representative to serve under your Health Care Proxy, as well as at least two successor Health Care Representatives. Express your desires if you are pregnant and if you wish to be an organ donor. Also discuss particular requests if you are currently diagnosed with a specific medical condition.

W. Your end-of-life care desires to be outlined in your Living Will. Include specific detail for your diseases, if any. Outline your wishes if you are pregnant and if you wish to be an organ donor.

5. At your meeting, tell your attorney *everything*. Share your concerns about a grandchild's drug use or a niece's out-of-wedlock child. Let your counselor know if any of your beneficiaries have disabilities or special needs. Be candid about your own health and well-being. Identify your estate planning goals, no matter what they are. This is not the time to hide information of any kind. Provide a specific time line for document completion.

6. Follow-up with your lawyer if you have any additional questions or concerns. If draft documents have not arrived when promised, call—and keep calling. Sadly, the client that keeps reminding her lawyer that she hasn't received her documents as promised usually receives them first!

7. When the draft documents arrive—READ THEM!!! Check the spelling of names. Be sure the individuals you've selected to serve as fiduciaries are listed in the correct order. Review the disposition of your assets, including the common disaster clause, to confirm that the provisions listed are what you want. They are called draft documents for a reason. They may contain errors, and it's your job to find them and alert your attorney to any mistakes that have been made.

8. After you've completed your review, call your lawyer to go over any changes. Set a date to sign your documents.

9. If you haven't already done so, bring copies of your beneficiary designations to your lawyer when you meet to sign your documents. Review them again with your attorney to see if any changes are required now that you've signed your estate planning documents. Discuss any other actions that are required on your part, such as opening accounts for Trusts, re-titling assets, and anything else you can think of.

10. Place your original documents in a firebox or important paper drawer in your home. Let your loved ones know where this information is located.

11. If you have minor children or are serving as Guardian for a disabled individual, prepare a Letter of Guidance to your named Guardians. Place this letter in your important paper drawer.

12. Prepare a memorandum or other document disposing of your personal property. This document should be in your own handwriting and list each item in detail, as well as the full name of the person to receive each item. Send a copy of your memorandum to your lawyer. Be sure to send another copy whenever you update your list. Keep the original in your important paper drawer.

13. Consider funeral planning. Leave your wishes for your funeral and obituary in your important paper drawer. Provide details if your funeral has been prepaid.

14. Leave a detailed Letter of Instruction for your loved ones. Your Letter of Instruction should include the following information.

    A. Names, addresses, and telephone numbers for your attorney, accountant, financial advisor, and other professionals.

    B. Names, addresses, and telephone numbers for everyone who should be notified of your death.

C. Location of your original Last Will and Testament and other legal documents, including deeds, Trust Agreements, original stock certificates, cemetery plot records, and titles to vehicles, boats, and other titled assets.

D. Location of income and gift tax returns.

E. Location of your safe deposit box and key.

F. List of bank and brokerage accounts and account numbers.

G. List of life insurance and annuity policies, policy numbers, and whereabouts of the original policies.

H. Contact information for organizations that may provide a death benefit, such as unions, the Veteran's Administration, and social organizations.

I. List of available employee and death benefits and your human resources contact information.

J. Details regarding any other assets you own or are entitled to.

K. List of your debts and payments that may be due.

L. Location of all account passwords or other access information, including your online service provider.

M. Location of any concealed items, including jewelry, sterling silver, or cash. Give your heirs a hint where to look.

15. Consider making annual exclusion or other gifts. Keep detailed records.

16. Review your documents at least every five years, or whenever you experience a major life event.

17. Fly first class now and then! You deserve it and it may be great estate planning!

Again, congratulations for taking charge of your affairs and working toward protecting your assets. It's a lot of work, I know; but it will provide you, and your loved ones, peace of mind and sound sleep once you're finished.

Suggested Resources

AARP—www.aarp.org

American Bar Association Lawyer Locator—
www.abanet.org/lawyerlocator/searchlawyer.html

American College of Trust and Estate Counsel—
www.actec.org

Funeral Consumers Alliance Web site—
www.funerals.org

Funeral Planning Information—
www.funeralinformation.net

Internal Revenue Service—www.irs.gov

Martindale-Hubbell Lawyer Locator—
www.martindale.com

National Academy of Elder Law Attorneys—
www.naela.com

Society of Financial Service Professionals—
www.financialpro.org

Veteran's Administration—www.va.gov

Glossary

Administrator   The individual or financial institution appointed by the courts to oversee the estate of a person who has died without a valid Will or without naming an Executor or Personal Representative; also referred to as an *Administratrix*.

Advance Directive for Health Care   A document that combines both the Living Will directives and Health Care Proxy selection into a single document.

Agent   The individual or individuals that you choose to make your financial and business decisions under a Power of Attorney; also called an *Attorney-in-Fact*.

Antibiotics   Drugs designed to fight infections that can be administered by mouth (PO), by the vein (IV), or by a feeding tube.

Artificially administered feeding and fluids   Sustenance provided to a person who cannot eat or drink on their own. There are several types of artificial feeding and fluids: Total Enteral Nutrition (using the intestinal tract to eat) through the use of a Nasogastric Tube (a feeding tube temporarily placed through a person's nose down to their stomach for liquefied food to be pumped); or a Gastric (or Duodenal or Jejunal) Tube (a feeding tube that is placed through the stomach or small intestine wall and out through the skin of the abdomen); and Total Parenteral Nutrition (providing nutrition by going around the intestinal tract using Intra Venous (IV) fluids or a larger venous catheter in a vein).

Asset Protection Trust   A Trust designed to provide creditor protection.

Beneficiary   Any person who receives proceeds from an estate, trust, insurance policy, or other asset.

Beneficiary designation   The form that allows you to select a particular individual or entity to receive the proceeds from an insurance policy, retirement account, or other asset.

Bequest   A small or specific gift made to an individual or charity in a Will or Trust, usually a dollar amount or specific item of property; also referred to as a *devise*.

By-pass Trust   A Trust designed to utilize an individual's applicable exclusion from estate tax by placing the exclusion amount in a trust for a surviving spouse.

Cardiopulmonary resuscitation (CPR)   A combination of rescue breathing and chest compressions delivered to patients when their heart is thought to stop beating (cardiac arrest). CPR can support a small amount of blood flow to the heart and brain to buy time if normal heart function can be restored.

Charitable Lead Trust   A charitable Trust that provides an income stream to a designated charity for a term of years, with the remainder of the trust passing to the trust Grantor or other individuals designated by the Grantor.

Charitable Remainder Trust   A charitable Trust which provides the trust income for a term of years or life to an individual, with the remainder of the trust passing to a designated charity.

Codicil   A properly executed legal document that changes part of an existing Will, without nullifying the entire Will.

Conservator   The individual appointed by a court to manage the financial affairs of an incapacitated person.

Credit shelter Trust   A Trust designed to utilize an individual's applicable exclusion from estate tax by placing the exclusion amount in a trust for a surviving spouse.

Decedent   An individual who has died.

Defibrillation   A process in which an electronic device gives an electric shock to the heart to reestablish normal contraction rhythms in a heart having dangerous abnormal beats (arrhythmia) or in cardiac arrest.

Devise   A small or specific gift made to an individual or charity in a Will or Trust, usually a dollar amount or specific item of property; also referred to as a *bequest.*

Disclaimer   The legal document a beneficiary executes to refuse, or say "no thank you" to a benefit under a Will or Trust.

Escheat   Property that passes to the state as a result of a person dying intestate (without a legal Will) and having no living relatives at the time of death.

Estate   All property and assets owned by an individual at death.

Estate administration   The process of settling the estate of a deceased person.

Estate planning   The process of ordering one's legal affairs to ensure the distribution of one's property and assets as one wants and wishes.

Executor   The individual or financial institution that carries out the provisions of a Will; also referred to as an *Executrix* or *Personal Representative*.

Family Limited Partnership (FLP)   A partnership entity that restricts ownership and marketability of its units and is often used for estate planning purposes as a means to transfer units, at a discounted value, to other individuals.

Fiduciary   An individual or financial institution acting for the benefit of an estate, Trust, or person; includes *Executor*, *Trustee*, *Administrator*, *Conservator*, and *Guardian*.

Fiduciary duty   The legal obligation of a fiduciary to act with trust and good faith.

Generation skipping transfer tax   A tax imposed on transfers that "skip" a generation. Tax is imposed at a rate of approximately 50% on transfers above the generation skipping transfer tax exclusion ($2,000,000 in 2008).

Generation Skipping Trust   A Trust designed to fully utilize an individual's exclusion from generation skipping transfer tax by placing the exclusion amount in a trust for grandchildren or more remote descendants.

Grantor Retained Annuity Trust   Also known as a GRAT, this is a trust for a term of years where the Grantor receives back a certain percentage of the trust each year with the balance passing to the remainder beneficiaries.

Gross estate   The total value of all of a Decedent's assets and items over which the Decedent had control.

Guardian   An individual granted the power to take care of the day-to-day needs and property of a person who is incapacitated or a minor.

Guardian ad litem   A special guardian appointed by a Court to protect the interests of a minor or incapacitated individual during a Court action.

Guardian of the person   The individual or entity responsible for a child or incapacitated person's welfare, custody, and personal care.

Guardian of the property   The individual or entity responsible for a child or incapacitated person's assets and financial affairs.

Health Care Proxy   A legal document that appoints an individual, also known as your *Health Care Representative*, to make your medical decisions for you if you are unable; also called a *Durable Power of Attorney for Health Care, Medical Power of Attorney*, or *Advance Directive for Health Care—Proxy Directive*.

Health Care Representative   Individual named to make your health care and medical decisions under a Health Care Proxy.

Holographic Will A Will written entirely in the handwriting of the person making the Will that isn't witnessed or notarized.

Incentive Trust A Trust with terms designed to give the trust beneficiary incentive to be a productive individual.

Income beneficiary The beneficiary currently entitled to the income and/or principal benefits of a Trust.

Intangible property Stocks, securities, business interests, patents, bank accounts, copyrights, and all other financial investments.

Intestate Dying without a valid Will.

Irrevocable A legal document that can't be changed or revoked.

Irrevocable Life Insurance Trust A Trust designed to be the owner and beneficiary of a life insurance policy.

Issue All individuals born of a common ancestor. Your children, grandchildren, and great-grandchildren (and so on) are your issue; also referred to as *descendants*.

Joint tenants Ownership of an undivided interest in a whole asset (such as a house or joint bank account) that, upon the death of one joint tenant, automatically passes to the other surviving joint tenants.

Lifetime beneficiary A beneficiary currently entitled to the income and/or principal benefits of a Trust for the beneficiary's lifetime.

Limited Liability Company (LLC) An entity that restricts ownership and marketability of its shares and is often used for estate planning purposes as a means to transfer shares, at a discounted value, to other individuals.

Living Will A legal document that outlines your wishes regarding your medical care at the end of life; also called an *Advance Directive for Health Care—Instruction Directive, Medical Directive,* or *Directive for Physicians.*

Outright distribution A distribution from an estate or Trust that passes without any strings or conditions.

Payable on death (POD) account A designation on a bank or brokerage account or other asset that provides that the asset passes to the named individual on the owner's death.

Per capita The division of an estate among a single branch of the family tree in which all members share and share alike. If, for example, you leave your estate to your children *per capita* and one of your children has already died, the deceased child's share would be split among your living children.

Per stirpes Division of an estate among all branches of a family tree. If you leave your estate to your children per stirpes and one of your children has already died, your deceased child's share passes to his or her children; also referred to as *by representation.*

Personal property Art, antiques, furniture, photographs, paintings, collections. In other words, everything you can touch and feel.

Personal Representative   The individual appointed by a Court to administer an estate; also called an *Executor* or *Administrator*.

Power of appointment   The ability to direct or control the ultimate beneficiaries of Trust assets. Depending upon the terms of the Trust document, a power of appointment may be exercised during life or at death in a Last Will and Testament. A power of appointment may be limited or general.

Power of Attorney   A legal document in which a Principal requests that an Agent make all financial decisions on the Principal's behalf. Powers of Attorney may be General, Springing, or Limited.

Principal   The individual signing a Power of Attorney, Health Care Proxy, and/or a Living Will.

Probate   Establishing the validity and authenticity of a Last Will and Testament before a judicial authority.

Qualified Domestic Trust (QDOT)   A Trust for the benefit of a spouse who is not a U.S. citizen.

Qualified Personal Residence Trust (QPRT)   A Trust owning real property that lasts for a term of years.

Qualified Terminable Interest Property (QTIP) Trust   A Trust for the benefit of a surviving spouse that qualifies for the marital deduction.

Real property   Land and whatever is attached to the land.

Remainder beneficiary   The beneficiary who receives the benefits from a Trust at the termination of the Trust.

Residue   The balance of an estate after the payment of all debts, taxes, expenses, bequests, and devises.

Respiratory Support   The administration of extra oxygen through various mechanisms such as High Flow Oxygen Therapy (oxygen given by face mask or nasal prongs or cannulas); Continuous Positive Airways Pressure (forcing oxygen into areas of the lungs being underutilized); Endotracheal Intubation and Ventilation (putting a tube into the mouth or nose of a person who cannot breathe on his or her own and having a machine breathe for the person); or a Tracheotomy (a surgical incision in the windpipe).

Revocable   A legal document that can be changed, amended, or cancelled.

Revocable Living Trust   A revocable Trust established during life for the benefit of the Grantor. Also called a *Grantor Trust* or *Living Trust.*

Section 529 plan   A tax-deferred education savings plan.

See-through Trust   A Trust with terms that allow the trust to qualify as a designated beneficiary of an Individual Retirement Account.

Surgery   Any invasive procedure or operation. Surgery may be minimal (such as the placement of a central line for IV access) or major (such as open heart surgery), or somewhere in between.

Tenants by the entirety   Joint ownership of property with a right of survivorship that is only between a husband and wife and today is usually associated only with land.

Tenants-in-common   Property ownership with other individuals that may or may not be equal, with the share of a co-tenant passing on his or her death pursuant to his or her Will or by the laws of intestacy.

Terminal health condition   A disease or state of being that is expected to end one's life within six months; also referred to as *end-stage*.

Testate   Dying with a valid Will.

Testator   Any individual who leaves a valid Will at the time of his or her death.

Trust   A separate, legal entity that holds property for another person's benefit (the beneficiary). An *inter vivos Trust* is established during life. A *testamentary Trust* is established at death.

Trustee   The individual or financial institution that administers a Trust.

Uniform Transfers to Minors Act (UTMA) or **Uniform Gifts to Minors Act (UGMA) Accounts**   Accounts opened in the name of a minor that become available to the minor at the age of majority (18 in some states, 21 in other states).

Will   A legal document in which a person disposes of property at death; short form of *Last Will and Testament*.

I N D E X

Numbers

FINANCIAL TIMES

In an increasingly competitive world, it is quality
of thinking that gives an edge—an idea that opens new
doors, a technique that solves a problem, or an insight
that simply helps make sense of it all.

We work with leading authors in the various arenas
of business and finance to bring cutting-edge thinking
and best-learning practices to a global market.

It is our goal to create world-class print publications
and electronic products that give readers
knowledge and understanding that can then be
applied, whether studying or at work.

To find out more about our business
products, you can visit us at www.ftpress.com.